Praise for *Asians in Ch* **ia**
whom Kenneth has developed, coached and
collaborated with, and are now in charge!

"A powerfully inspiring and practical guide to being a better leader. As a benefactor of Kenneth's leadership and mentorship, I have seen first-hand how he leads and motivates high-performing organisations that operate with purpose. This book encapsulates everything he has taught me over the years. I only wish he had written it earlier!"
– Benjamin Boh, McDonald's Managing Director, Singapore

"As a role model for Asian leaders, Kenneth broke the glass ceiling of MNCs by stepping out of his comfort zone and staying laser-focused on strategies. This book is essentially a bible for Asian leaders to thrive, powered by Kenneth's all-encompassing management insight."
– Randy Lai, McDonald's CEO, Hong Kong

"I have known Kenneth to be an empathetic, visionary leader over the many years of coaching and mentoring me. He has always challenged me to adopt a bigger and bolder vision for the business and the organisation. The leadership blindspots and practices discussed in *Asians in Charge* have benefited my team and helped me lead with more confidence. I hope the book offers you as many 'A-ha' moments as it has me."
– Sylvia Tao, McDonald's Managing Director, Taiwan

"An authentic and comprehensive look at successfully adopting an impactful leadership style, offering practical real-life learnings from a hands-on CEO. Kenneth's leadership legacy reflects his philosophy of driving business with purpose; his best bets will be a great guide for all who aspire to make it big in corporate Asia."
– Smita Jatia, McDonald's Managing Director, India

"I can absolutely relate to the authenticity and practical tips shared in *Asians in Charge* because these learnings originate from Kenneth's personal success story, as well as my own personal journey to become an Asian in charge of a multinational business. *Asians in Charge* will provide inspiration and motivation for Asian and global leaders, and allow global companies to have better empathy and understanding of Asian talent as they expand in the region."
– Azmir Jaafar, McDonald's Managing Director &
Operating Partner, Malaysia

"In close to two decades with McDonald's, I have witnessed Kenneth's leadership in defining a bold ambition to steer his teams with his stirring plans and making these plans come to life, whether in better times or in crisis. He has consistently placed the highest priority when it comes to developing his people to become better leaders for the organisation. Kenneth is the epitome of an awe-inspiring leader."
– Margot Torres, McDonald's Managing Director, Philippines

ASIANS
IN CHARGE

How to Earn Your Place at the Leadership Table

KENNETH CHAN

Marshall Cavendish
Business

Published in 2022 by Marshall Cavendish Business
An imprint of Marshall Cavendish International

Other Marshall Cavendish Offices:
Marshall Cavendish Corporation, 800 Westchester Ave, Suite N-641, Rye Brook, NY 10573, USA • Marshall Cavendish International (Thailand) Co Ltd, 253 Asoke, 16th Floor, Sukhumvit 21 Road, Klongtoey Nua, Wattana, Bangkok 10110, Thailand • Marshall Cavendish (Malaysia) Sdn Bhd, Times Subang, Lot 46, Subang Hi-Tech Industrial Park, Batu Tiga, 40000 Shah Alam, Selangor Darul Ehsan, Malaysia

Marshall Cavendish is a registered trademark of Times Publishing Limited

National Library Board, Singapore Cataloguing in Publication Data

Name(s): Chan, Kenneth.
Title: Asians in charge : how to earn your place at the leadership table / Kenneth Chan.
Description: Singapore : Marshall Cavendish Business, 2022.
Identifier(s): ISBN 978-981-5009-87-3 (paperback)
Subject(s): LCSH: Leadership--Asia. | Management--Asia.
Classification: DDC 658.4092--dc23

Printed in Singapore

To my colleagues over my 30-year career –
I am forever grateful for your wisdom,
kindness and friendship

To my wife, Elena –
you are my heart, soul and joy

CONTENTS

Part 3: Leadership in a VUCA World

FOREWORD

PHYLLIS CHEUNG
CEO, McDonald's China

It has been ten years since I assumed the role of Managing Director and, after all that time, I am now referred to as a well-seasoned CEO. Kenneth has had a big impact on my professional career and personal growth. Much of his management philosophy and the practices that he covers in this book have been deeply embedded in our China organisation even till today.

My leadership journey with Kenneth can be divided into four phases.

The first phase was when I was the Chief Marketing Officer (CMO) at McDonald's China and he was Managing Director at McDonald's Singapore. I was astounded by his daring and breakthrough concept of introducing home delivery in Singapore and offering it 24 hours a day, 7 days a week! This was in 2004, before home delivery became a pervasive part of the F&B industry (only the pizza boys were providing wide-scale delivery then). Kenneth had successfully earned the trust from our global stakeholders to try something that was far from the norm for McDonald's then, and to put in the investment required to build out this new convenience model. The results were outstanding right out of the starting

gate, and the delivery business has since experienced dou-
ble-digit growth over 18 consecutive years. This success
inspired the adoption of delivery throughout the APMEA
region and, today, McDelivery has become a critical growth
driver for the entire McDonald's system. Separately, I would
also look forward to when Kenneth would present his plans
or share learnings in our regional meetings as it was always
one of the more anticipated and inspirational sessions.

The second phase was when Kenneth became CEO of
McDonald's China. He crafted the first Team China Vision
that energised our local organisation and captured the imagi-
nation of the global McDonald's enterprise with our exciting
and bold growth plans. He shattered the glass ceiling for our
mainland Chinese talents and raised up the first generation of
locally groomed leaders. Many of those leaders now hold top
executive positions within the McDonald's China business
and in other external companies. It was during this phase
that Kenneth provided me the opportunity to embark on
a succession plan to eventually replace him as CEO China.
Apart from providing the opportunity for me to move out
of what was a critical CMO role then to take on a General
Management line position to get more field experience, I also
recall a pivotal coaching moment which we shared. During
the tenure of my succession development training, I was subsequently offered the dual opportunity to take on the COO
role in China, or to take on the Managing Director role in
Singapore. I wanted to remain in China and thought the

COO role would be a great stepping stone to my subsequent CEO position. Staying in China and the system I was familiar with was also within my comfort zone. I recall Kenneth telling me that both opportunities were fantastic ones, and that he could sure use the help for the work we had to do in China. But he also pointed out that the Managing Director role in Singapore would provide me an invaluable learning opportunity on how to adapt to new environments, how to lead new organisations, and how to be resilient whilst facing new challenges. Most importantly, he mentioned that while the COO position in China carried heavy responsibility, there would be no substitute for gaining the experience and understanding the leadership burden of taking on the Number 1 role – being the ultimate decision-maker, being fully accountable for the business results, and being responsible for people's jobs and welfare. I did finally choose the Singapore MD role and flourished in the work, achieved strong results, and gained lots of practical experience along the way. I expanded my role to also provide regional cover for Malaysia, and eventually made my way back to take on the successor role in China. I appreciated the advice and also the generosity that Kenneth showed in allowing me to make the move to Singapore even though I knew he could have used my help as his right-hand person in China when we were fast expanding.

The third phase was when Kenneth was the Division President of Greater China. As a team, we faced and navigated our way through one of the biggest brand trust crises in our history (Kenneth shares more about this incident in the book). He showed us how to calmly (but with a sense of urgency) organise ourselves to get out of this difficult situation, whilst bringing to life our company values throughout this period of adversity. The consistent empathy and engagement of the entire system resulted in all our suppliers, franchisees and employees emerging even more united and energised coming out of the crisis, and with a renewed and unwavering commitment to win the future.

The fourth phase was when Kenneth became a Licensee Partner, a mentor and a life-long friend. When Kenneth passed the baton to me in 2015, he kept reminding me, "You are now the father and the mother of the company. Make sure you take care of the people." We continue to learn from each other till today and have each other's backs.

Kenneth truly cares for the people and always strives to provide servant leadership. In pouring his wealth of wisdom into this book, I know he hopes to offer his readers an organisational-stewardship framework, and to get better prepared to become a more effective and competitive global leader.

I was filled with reflective moments when reading this book during the Shanghai lockdown. The ideas are highly relevant and practical to the contextual challenge of leadership today. I hope you will enjoy reading and learning from this book as much as I have.

It's Time

"We face neither East nor West: we face forward."
KWAME NKRUMAH

"WE DO ALL THE WORK, and they take all the credit! There is a lot of talk, but we seem to be the ones getting down to all the action."

How many times have you heard the same grouse from Asian managers about their expat bosses or foreign counterparts? Whether this is a fair or unfair sentiment, the reality is that Western or foreign expatriates continue to be entrusted with the top positions in multinational companies (MNCs). Even more exasperating is the fact that this happens often in Asia, where we should have the know-how and advantage to do better by now.

But this book is certainly not about "us" versus "them". All of us in Asia have benefited tremendously from the experience of Western management and leadership theory. There is great value in what Western innovation, values, cultures, and management skills can bring to the table, and there is no doubt that these embedded ideas will continue to form the basis of how we operate in increasingly complex business environments. In the absence of a stronger pipeline of qualified Asian leaders, though, this import of foreign talent remains a practical stop-gap approach.

As more multinational corporations rapidly expand into international markets, the perpetual debate remains over whether all businesses can, and should, use the same successful global playbook to win the local marketplace.

In theory, that question has been asked and answered. People all over the world certainly have some of the same wants and needs that remain universal. How they get to those wants and needs, though – that happens in a myriad of different ways. There are dramatic as well as subtle differences in attitudes and behaviours as we move across continents. This is particularly true of the diversity found in Asia. Thus, every in-market business leader necessarily must strive for insightful local relevancy to adapt their business model to. Without it, they would not be able to engage effectively with the local consumer and workforce. The right local leaders would also be able to capitalise on these subtle differences to drive not just generic, but optimal performance.

In practice, however, I have observed many multinational businesses wrestling to find sustained and consistent footing in Asia. A large part of the time is wasted behind the continued reliance on expat leaders who have been parachuted in, turnstile fashion, to get the job done. There is a repetition of the steep learning curve as expats deploy into new markets, adapt to new cultures, and conduct business in languages foreign to them. There is also a natural bias from the expats to transplant their own set of cultural norms and values in their business dealings that sometimes come off as extremely foreign to the local market stakeholders. I say this for myself as well, having been an expat in overseas markets and with first-hand experience dealing with my strengths and deficiencies.

Why then do MNCs continue to fly in expats to do the job? Because there is a dearth of senior local Asian talent that is entrusted to take over the leadership mantle. This trend will unfortunately continue, and more effort and steadfast commitment will be required to develop and entrust Asian leaders with these positions, be it in the emerging Asian markets or even in the more developed ones. Clearly, all of us in Asia need to play our part. This cannot be an entitlement. There remains a gap in awareness of how Asian leaders behave and what we can do to help develop more well-rounded leadership and stewardship skills.

Evolve or Fade Away

I wrote this book to explain what Asian leaders need to do to fill the positions that expats currently occupy – how to operate at a higher level, how to gain trust, and how to be better business stewards compared to the current operating behaviour that is biased mostly towards execution.

I have close affinity with this topic as I consider myself a reluctant and insecure Asian leader who had to work – and continues to work – my way out of some of the common shortfall behaviours that I will share in this book. It was difficult for me, and my desire is to make this journey a bit easier for our next set of global Asian leaders.

I hope that this book will also help kickstart a more concerted effort to get Asians to compete successfully in multinational and/or global business environments, with a first step in Asia. Asians have significant strengths in work discipline, but also some obvious blind spots that need to be corrected before global stakeholders will want to pass them the mantle of top leadership positions. In the following chapters, we explore the behaviours that will allow Asian leaders to first be noticed and considered, and subsequently be entrusted with the top jobs in MNCs.

Many Asian businesses are – or soon will be – multinational businesses themselves, thus they will likewise have to manage diverse workforces in markets outside of their own. Just imagine the reverse situation of an Asian expat trying to manage an entrenched business in the U.S. market to optimum. It is clearly possible, but would that necessarily be the best choice? If we can develop a framework through which we engender trust and alignment for a global company *without* boxing-in the markets under one set of values, cultural norms or approaches, then we can unleash the true potential of local leaders leading their local businesses. At the same time, we can also mitigate the mistakes that the international go-to-market journey inevitably brings along with it through cultural missteps rooted in shallow market understanding.

This book is targeted at leaders who are on the cusp of breakthrough at the most senior positions. Since there are never definitive solutions to the practice of leadership, the ideas in this book represent observations and timely reminders for the reader to reflect on. I do generalise the subject matter quite a bit – with the intent to polarise and highlight the issues more aggressively, to create better awareness of our behavioural tendencies, and to rally all of us towards remedial action.

Of course, I acknowledge that no two Asian leaders or leadership styles are ever the same. I also acknowledge that there are Asian leaders who are clear outliers, already helming global corporations and engaged in diverse regional roles. I do believe, however, that if you are an Asian executive trying to fit and grow within the increasingly global business world, the ideas in this book are substantive and relevant. They are based on practical experience formed over my 30 years of working at all levels in Fortune 500 multinational companies, and from my own story of finding my place within these organisations. The lessons are also drawn from the hundreds of leaders around Asia whom I have had the privilege to work with, learn from, observe, and coach.

But Who Am I?

Still, you may wonder, who am I to speak with any authority on this subject? As an Asian who has been operating in a multinational business world, *I am that guy!*

I have successfully helmed a Fortune 500 multinational company through its fastest expansion period in Asia, winning significant market share and building a high-performing sustainable organisation. I led the McDonald's China business as CEO for close to seven years and held a concurrent appointment as Division President of Greater China (and following that, Greater Asia). During this tenure, I was the highest-ranking Asian within McDonald's at the time. Being long in the minority whilst occupying senior leadership level positions at multinationals, the areas I touch on in this book come from wide-ranging observations through my decades of work and interactions.

I took over the China business at a time when there was impetus for us to expand at a more rapid pace after years of cautious but judicious penetration of the marketplace. Comparisons in the quick-service restaurant industry would always pit our brand and business model against KFC, who had been extremely successful in growing their China business. But I always felt that we could do better. So, I set out a determined plan to do so with my team.

My team and I were able to set a clear and inspiring vision, marshal significant resources and capital, and build a winning organisation to lead the fastest period of expansion of the brand in China. Most importantly, our global stakeholders trusted us with this vision and execution, and with the capital required for investment. We returned that trust with solid results, staying aligned, and by being visible and transparent in all the steps that we took. I will share more on the leadership principles underlying this entire experience later in the book.

From the opening of its first outlet in 1990, it took McDonald's 18 years to build the first 1,000 restaurants in China. My team and I took just five years to build the next 1,000. More importantly, we established a solid foundation for future growth (as this book is written, China is expected to get to 4,500 restaurants by year end). This was accompanied by an unprecedented organisation expansion from 50,000 employees to 150,000 and growing, a doubling of revenues and profit, achieving brand and market share leadership in the top-tier cities, and a structural ownership shift towards franchising.

We were also the only company in China at the time to be conferred the Aon Hewitt Best Employer Award four consecutive times, which speaks to the leadership team's focus on people, engagement, and talent development that we saw as critical success factors for sustainable growth. Our field leaders in China are now 100% local, and the senior executive leadership team has been transformed from a 100% expat team to one that is close to 70% local and growing.

Beyond business success, there were also significant challenges and crises that one would expect from a VUCA (Volatile, Uncertain, Complex, Ambiguous) environment like China. The ability to manage through and overcome these situations reflects the ability to marshal and deploy diverse resources as well as engender trust from global stakeholders to make critical decisions. Given the volatility in Asia, and especially in the emerging markets, having a strong level of trust is essential in the quick resolution of these issues. I will share some of these case studies in this book.

The ability to manage the business on a strategic level while achieving execution speed and excellence is an invaluable leadership combination that Asian leaders can aspire to. But just as important is the ability to bring stakeholders along on the journey and establish absolute trust behind the immense responsibility of the proper stewardship of the business, the brand, its capital, and the people.

Are you ready to be a part of the Asian leadership evolution? Let's begin by identifying and understanding the problems inherent first, before we get down to the strategies in Part 2 of this book.

PART 1

Identifying the Problem

CHAPTER 1

Disrupt Tradition

"To avoid criticism, say nothing,
do nothing, be nothing."
ARISTOTLE

I N HIS RECENT BOOK, *The Future is Asian*, author and geopolitical specialist Parag Khanna reminds us that Asia will house "five billion people, two-thirds of the world's mega-cities, one-third of the global economy, two-thirds of global economic growth, thirty of the Fortune 100, six of the ten largest banks, eight of the ten largest armies, five nuclear powers, massive technological innovation, the newest crop of top-ranked universities. Asia is also the world's most ethnically, linguistically and culturally diverse region of the planet, eluding any remotely meaningful generalisation beyond the geographic label itself. Even for Asians, Asia is dizzying to navigate."[1]

As more global businesses move towards Asia to capitalise on the rapid growth in the region (the pandemic notwithstanding, the IMF projects 6.3% growth in 2022 for Asia compared to 4.9% for the world[2]), there is a pressing need to develop senior Asian talent that can fill the top leadership pipeline and better anchor these businesses and organisations in the local marketplace. Asian businesses are also expanding their scope regionally, and have found themselves urgently needing to adapt to the new world we have found ourselves in. Finding the right leadership talent to navigate businesses through these complexities remains the biggest opportunity in being able to grow at a more aggressive pace.

Asian leaders managing international businesses in their local countries have the potential to offer the longer-term advantages of providing in-market stability, cost-effectiveness, and the local knowledge and relevance to win decisively in the nuanced marketplace. They would naturally have the cultural intuition and insight to more effectively reach out and engage with the local consumer and local workforce. They are also better able to adapt global strategies to the appropriate regional or local context.

But this potential must evolve to actualisation. Asian leaders today typically have a keen bias towards top-down management, in other words the tendency to micromanage and to push quickly for execution and results. While this remains a key differentiated strength in moving projects fast and efficiently, it also represents a weakness of the Asian leadership brand in being able to provide better thought out, longer-term strategic and collaborative leadership to the business.

Global businesses appointing top leadership positions in their critical Asian markets need to be able to trust and see that the local business not only does well for the near term, but also for the longer term, with a clear vision of how the business, brand and organisation can be sustained and taken forward. They need a business leader who can navigate through and deliver precisely on this balance. In-market leaders also need to exhibit responsible capital management, compliance, and the ability to articulate the dynamics of the business succinctly. Western leaders generally tend to take more time and care in managing this broader aspect of business stewardship.

The Watchouts in Asian Leadership

None of this came naturally to me. In my teens, my family moved to the U.S., and I had to juggle culture shock along with the typical growing pains of young adulthood. I learnt to adapt and thrive in my new environment, and I continued to build upon these skills as I made my way through life, continuously going back and forth through the Asian and Western spheres.

There were some cultural lenses from my growing up years that I had to recognise and mitigate, which remain formative to my character and behaviour. You may recognise these innate mindsets in yourself too, and they can be stumbling blocks to your growth as a leader because they often get in the way of putting leadership theory into practice. Being aware of these cultural mind traps, I have had to check myself and filter out these behaviours in my leadership choices to be more effective when navigating in international business environments.

Watchout 1: Deference to Elders

Most of us were born in traditional Asian households, where great value is placed on respecting parents and elders. Filial piety is based on hierarchical relationships in which parents and the elderly rank higher than children or younger family members. This sense of hierarchical respect also carries through to other aspects of life, where authority figures or people in positions of power are accorded high respect.

Over the course of my career, I have come to recognise the positives of this cultural approach – showing respect, being well-mannered, and having a sense of civility is never passé. But the downside of it cannot be ignored: the tendency to always wait for direction; having blind faith, and unearned respect, in the wrong people; overly deferring to authority figures; and, especially, not challenging obvious mistakes.

The Mitigator

Blindly following directives, just because they come from the boss, is probably one of my biggest bugbears. I have always believed that every part of the organisation should strive for self-sufficiency and provide thought, business, and people leadership over their respective areas of responsibility. I have always been a bit bemused when I walk into a meeting and find a group of people sitting in front of me with notepads in hand, asking, "OK, boss, what do we do now?"

I dislike using the word "boss" to describe my position.

I want independence in thinking from my team and have therefore implemented certain ways of working to mitigate such top-down approaches to leading. So first things first, stop thinking of yourself as the "boss", and get your team to stop referring you by that moniker.

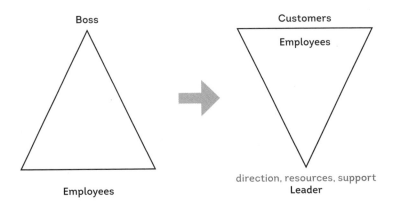

This classic diagram illustrates how most Asian-based companies operate. The left triangle is probably what most people are used to, with the "boss" right on top and his or her subordinates forming the base of the triangle. The triangle on the right, where customers and employees are at the top, is what we should aspire to in order to build a living, motivated and self-sufficient organisation. You may say it's a triangle that's upside-down. Many refer to it as one that is actually right-side-up.

When an Asian company is run by a dominant boss (left triangle), everyone follows the leader, waits for his or her instructions, and offers loyalty in return for security and compensation – and sometimes out of fear. The organisation and employees tend to defer big strategic decisions to the all-knowing boss, leaving plans not fully transparent and accountability unclear. This follow-the-leader top-down organisation approach thrives on obedient and subservient employees who navigate a safe path through their careers. They don't play an aggressive game to win, but take a cautious path so as not to lose. There is little incentive to contribute more than necessary, to develop and grow to take on more responsibility and make more decisions, or to drive for change, as that would clearly be an act of sticking out your neck unnecessarily. Why bother with all that when the direction is always coming from the top, and questioning decisions becomes a bad career move? In their minds, "As long as I do what the boss wants, don't stick my neck out too much, I will have security and be compensated for my obedience and loyalty. No need for me to stretch too much."

But who are the ones who are really the closest to the customer and at the front end of the business? Especially in this day and age, shouldn't they have a say in how the business is run, provide insight into customers, offer ideas for improvement, be in charge of their own units? The right-side-up triangle reflects this operating and cultural environment, where employees are empowered to lead, manage and run their respective parts of the business. They are self-motivated, self-led and self-sufficient. The role of management and leaders in this environment is to provide the strategic direction (which is co-created, ideally), resources, policy, training and development, and motivation for everyone in the organisation to succeed. In this model, employees would understand their transparent goals and targets, understand how compensation impacts the achievement of these, and are self-motivated to drive for better results. In their minds, "I know where success lies, and I know what I need to do to achieve those goals and get compensated for it. I will offer my best contribution and strive for more."

In McDonald's, our crew and their managers in the restaurants are closest to the customer, not those of us working in the HQ office. Each restaurant unit has a Restaurant General Manager who is competent and well-trained, and in charge of their million-dollar business (we don't think of it much, but the revenue in our restaurants make our employees small and medium enterprise (SME) operators). Each restaurant employs crew from all walks of life, operates the "daily miracle" of opening the restaurant, offers consistent and high-quality food and service, and almost always does so at a level of efficiency we take for granted.

I have a saying to my office folks, as a constant reminder that our job is to face and fully support the restaurants: "We don't see a single customer in the office, and we don't make a single cent in the office. It's all at the restaurants." Covid-19 made this notion even more apparent as frontliners all over the world bravely stayed in position in the field while the rest of us in the office had the luxury of working from home. Our hats off to them.

Your staff must be empowered to take the initiative and lead without having to take specific directions from you for every single move. They are likely the ones who have on-the-ground knowledge of the day-to-day. They need to be able to think on their feet and pivot where necessary. A squadron that relies only on the general to give orders will be at loss when communication devices fail, for example.

Our main role as leaders is to provide strategic direction, resources, motivation, and recognition. With my own direct reports, I have them each write down on one page their clear goals and strategies for the year. It is necessary that they do this one-pager so that they can articulate clearly, and succinctly, what *they* wish to achieve. Thereafter, we have monthly sit-downs to review their progress. Through it all, I function as their support base, not as their commander micromanaging.

In fact, the moment they feel that I am micromanaging or that they need to be micromanaged, it will be clear to me that we are in a spot of trouble. Empower your staff and watch them be more agile. Working in this manner energises everyone, and the organisation becomes a living, breathing one that can act and adapt appropriately instead of continually getting stuck at roadblocks, waiting for instructions.

As Asian leaders, are we able and willing to empower our teams to get the job done? Are we committed to providing the learning and development resources for our teams to be self-sufficient, high-performing units? Are we able to create a culture where everybody has a say and a point-of-view — all behind the common goal of continuous improvement?

Watchout 2: Rote Learning

Like most students of my generation, I settled for rote learning to move through the education system and pass examinations. My days in primary and part of secondary school in Singapore were filled with memorisation and textbook study. As an example, learning Mandarin at that time was focused around memorising passages of Chinese text and spewing back the contents in the hope that some of the words, usage and context would live on in our long-term memory. Meaning, context and understanding took second place to the required outcome of verbalising and writing.

Clearly, much has changed and improved in the decades since, but this bias towards rote learning and good grades continues to feature prominently in the Asian education system. This in turn shapes the kind of workers and leaders we get in the working world once they have matured to adulthood. It unfortunately holds back a lot of Asians from being able to participate in dialogue naturally and comfortably. It makes them less likely to think on their feet, to engage in discussions, and to spar with ideas or concepts. Asians are much less vocal in meetings and contribute less to the ideation process, much to the chagrin of their Western bosses.

Creativity and innovation in delivering thought-out and robust solutions are also not as forthcoming, and thus there is an unfortunate tendency towards copied ideas, obvious and mediocre thinking that can be easily bested in quick time, and a herd mentality in idea acceptance.

In Asia, governments also tend to be more involved in the daily lives of their citizenry. Policies are for the most part well laid out and often mandated, and with whatever varying level of trust in the authorities, we go about our lives adhering to this overarching structure. In some circumstances, this type of social compact bodes well in bringing people together towards a common cause – during the Covid-19 pandemic, it was easier for Asian countries to implement and get the cooperation of their citizenry for tough measures like universal masking and the various safe management rules. But in other circumstances, this patriarchal structure falls short in creating the right environment for innovation, out-of-the-box thinking, and bolder iteration of ideas.

The Mitigator

The tendency, then, is for a lot of Asians to stay on a safe and charted course with little impetus to level up towards more innovative or creative solutions, or to take more risks. Wherever you find this tendency, nip it in the bud. Ask yourself: "If someone else were in my position now, would she be able to engage more robustly? Would she be able to offer better alternatives? Would she be able to offer more creative solutions?" If the answer is yes, then strive to get out of your comfort zone. Step back and think about how you can broaden your perspective and deliver ideas with a stronger growth mindset.

With my own team, whenever I find myself amid a crowd of only one perspective, which everyone is remarkably in agreement with, I try and play the antagonist. I voice the contrary view to get the ball rolling, and soon enough, others will chime in. If you do not do this, you will find it out sooner or later in the corridor chat afterwards. Asians tend to be afraid of being the one voicing a different opinion, and sometimes those very opinions are crucial to solving a problem at hand.

This is also where the Western style of doing business might be worth borrowing. Make it a habit after each discussion to process the meeting and review what was discussed. How did the meeting go? Did we offer solid (or just mediocre) ideas? And did we build upon them with robust discussion to weed out better solutions? Sometimes, a bit of time is all that is needed to get the minds to process all the information, and you may well discover some valuable information that would not have been unearthed had you simply taken it for granted that everyone agrees with everything that has been tabled.

Watchout 3: Fear of Failure

Much has already been said about Asian tiger parents and their strict demands for their children to succeed. Consequently, Asians on a whole tend to have a deep-rooted fear of failure – or more commonly referred to in Asia as "losing face" – and that is something that the wider world has taken notice of, especially in business.[3] Fear of failure also keeps people away from taking risks, and when you have business leaders too afraid of making any mistakes to take their company further, you have a group of people that will never be entrusted with top-level positions that require bold decision-making.

I remember very clearly a lesson I learnt early on in my career. I was a young brand manager for a diaper brand and was supposed to do a product demonstration. We had these paper cut-outs that we would use to show our customers, demonstrating with weights and measures how well our brand of diapers worked in absorbing liquid. But our latest product didn't quite hit the mark, so I had trouble demonstrating that it was an efficacious product. However, instead of reporting to my boss that it was a failure, I embellished the events and said that everything went well at the demonstration. Unfortunately for me, someone else went back to the bosses to tell them that the product was not as good as it should have been – you can just imagine how that worked out for me. Rather than acknowledging the root cause being the deficient product, I had taken the failed demonstration as a personal shortcoming. My time and energy could have been better spent working on the problem and contributing to product improvement. Instead, I made a fool of myself and lost credibility. All for the sake of saving face. Never again.

In the senior leadership positions I have taken on these many years, I have always tried to deliver on bold strategies to change the trajectory of the business, change the culture of our internal organisation, and change the impressions of our customers. In every instance, I could not tell you up-front if these directions would 100% work and lead to success. The bolder the strategy or the deeper the transformation, the greater the element of risk, either through failed strategic moves or because we are not able to bring the organisation along. As Asian leaders, we must acknowledge that this is the price of leadership: we live and die by the direction we set for the business. Let's clearly lead with a rational and educated mind, but be sure to also lead with a bold and courageous mindset.

The Mitigator

Failure should not be feared. Face it and face the truth of it, because that is the only way you are going to move on and be better. Failure can be the teacher that will help you to understand what you did wrong and what changes you must make to get it right the next time. It is important to manage this fear because anything worth doing carries with it a great deal of risk. The only caveat to this is that you must be sure that you have learnt the lesson that failure is teaching you. To keep on failing instead – now that is a matter for concern.

I have also learnt that being candid and frank in conversations with my team from the outset is extremely helpful in cultivating efficiency in our management interactions and being clear about the areas we do well in and those where we continue to have opportunities. In Asian culture, this frankness is sometimes off-putting. But if your team understands and trusts that all these comments come from a place of respect and come from a place of wanting to be helpful and not hurtful, then I think over time the team looks to these conversations as solid coaching and learning interactions. In time, they will also return candid feedback of their own.

Watchout 4: Lack of Strategising

There is a tendency among some Asians to focus on the obvious ideas and then immediately jump to execution. They think less about robust, competitive strategy, how to run the business in the long-term, and how to behave as a business steward. People with traits like this do not ascend to higher leadership roles because they are unable to articulate the organisation's purpose and doings in broader terms and cannot shepherd the organisation through more transformational changes.

Imagine you are a CEO in New York, and you are in talks with the person managing your business in the field in

China, but this person cannot clearly communicate her plans. Everything sounds suspiciously peachy-keen, there is lots of busy activity going on, but the key strategies that lead to success are not apparent. It's difficult in this scenario to place full trust in this field manager, or to provide more allowance for capital expenditure, as it's unclear what track the business is on. You would probably cancel all your appointments and fly down to the field to sort things out yourself!

The Mitigator: A Case Study

China was not at the top of my list of countries to work in. The first time I was offered the opportunity to head up the McDonald's business there was in 2007, but I turned it down because I was not confident that I could take on such a big and pivotal role.

Subsequently, I went through a global leadership programme which helped me rationalise my fears and surrounded me with other colleagues who were also positioned to take on bigger roles. I then decided I was ready for the challenge. At the end of 2008, I indicated that I was open to working in China, thinking that it would be two years before I went there. To my amazement, I was asked to go almost immediately. In January 2009, I found myself in Shanghai in the middle of winter and tasked with expanding McDonald's presence in China.

The notion then was that since China was such a massive country with a population of 1.3 billion people, the biggest opportunity to offer our unique food and services to the growing middle class was to aggressively open more restaurants in the right locations. The inherited strategy at the time I entered the business could have been stronger. We were expanding at a much slower pace than our key competitor, KFC. We had 26 McDonald's offices located all over China – trying to capture the opportunity in the different tier markets – but we were not winning in any one of those cities. Most of our money was made in the four key Tier 1 cities (Beijing, Shanghai, Guangzhou and Shenzhen) and yet our market penetration in those huge cities was low. There was also lesser consideration on building a proper infrastructure for restaurant development and to leverage supply chain, talent, marketing, and technology. Our strategy was not focused or robust enough to win the marketplace.

So when I came on board, we took a step back to properly understand what the key issues were. I determined that we needed some help to formulate a much more robust, longer-term strategy based on data and facts, and thus we sought the help of market consultants to help us frame where we needed to be. The way I saw it, if we got the foundation right, it would allow us to run faster and be more planful in how we went forward thereafter. (As an aside, the value in consulting market specialists is often overlooked in Asian businesses. Seeking expert help wherever needed, especially in factually understanding the marketplace and customers, offers a more objective approach to developing strategy for the organisation. Asian businesses tend to be wary of using these external resources.)

At the time when we were formulating a go-forward strategy for China, the larger McDonald's system – which already operated 32,000 restaurants – had embarked on a "Not just Bigger, but Better" mantra, the notion being that growth could not just be derived from new restaurant expansion, that we had to deliver stronger organic and same-store growth by modernising the business, engaging and being more relevant to our customers and ensuring that we built the brand and brand trust.

Given the huge geography, the rapidly growing middle class, and the proliferation of multinational brands all making their entry into the marketplace, we framed our China market-penetration strategy under the mantra of "Bigger, Better, Faster". Similar to the overall system strategy, we definitely had to execute our core business Better. But because this was China, we also had to grow Bigger. And because of the heated competition in securing good real estate locations, we had to capture this opportunity Faster. This broad mantra allowed us to capture the essence of our strategy and promote easy understanding and application down the organisation ranks.

- Under "Bigger", our key focus would clearly be on significant new restaurant growth to capture the marketplace, and our strategies would have to guide us on where to grow, what restaurant formats (e.g., drive-thrus, malls) to deploy, and what organisation and systems/tools we would need to make this happen.

- Under "Better", our key focus would be on building the McDonald's brand in China. The strategies would guide us on which target consumers (e.g., families) to would focus on, what menu offerings and value proposition would resonate, what brand extensions (e.g., McCafé, Delivery, Dessert Kiosks) might help deliver sustained organic growth. We would also make sure that we ran great restaurants with robust systems and unmatched service.

- Under "Faster", our key consideration was building a solid infrastructure which would then allow the pace of growth to be accelerated. We would be guided by strategies around staffing, talent management and development, supply chain, and partner excellence to ensure sustained food quality and safety as the business got significantly bigger; logistics to support the efficient distribution of goods throughout the vast geography; IT and technology to allow business systems to be kept simple; and the use of data analytics to provide business insights.

With this approach, we set out a core-market strategy which outlined that we would be in the top 11 cities in China first. We made a deliberate choice to pause our openings in any other cities until we had those 11 appropriately populated with the right number of restaurants. The reasoning behind this strategy was that those cities were where most of the middle-class consumers were. It also led to efficiency on various fronts. For example, if we had 100 stores in Shanghai at that time, and then doubled it to 200 stores, the efficiency in advertising would be much better for us as we would be able to generate more revenue with the same spend. The same benefit of efficiency can be seen in other key areas like supply chain and logistics, as well as training and development resources.

Once we got that into scale, we revised our strategy and went into Tier 3 markets, Tier 4, and so on. There was constant revisiting and revising of our strategies depending on what was going on. We also supplemented the core strategies with a franchising strategy to tackle the markets that would be very tough for us to get into, like Yunnan province, and far-away remote markets like Heilongjiang. In this strategy, we would engage franchisees who were far more well-versed in those local markets than we were, and they would use their resources and personnel to expand for us.

It might have taken a bit more time at the beginning to organise all that thinking, but we actually ran faster and more efficiently because everything was set up to support those strategies we formulated. Years later, the team today continue to use these strategies to expand further in China.

Of course, we were met with a few objections at the beginning from people who were not used to these strategies. "There is such great opportunity in this Tier 4 city, why don't we open restaurants there now?" And of course, we could, but we chose not to, because we knew the more sustainable strategy called for an expansion plan that resembled an inkblot as opposed to a scattergun approach. People grumbled over having to close offices in some of the other cities when we were focusing on only the top 11 cities. They fussed over constraints with headcount as most of the allocation was first given to building the real estate and development team. Strategy is about the allocation of resources, time and money; the discipline to stick with this allocation to get the best and fastest result is imperative, even if it meets resistance. That's where good communication, and bringing people along comes in – topics I will cover later in the book.

Grounded by Heritage, Lifted by Possibilities

By highlighting Asian "watchouts" in this chapter, I am not in the least dismissing the strength of our cultural or environmental programming. I am extremely proud to have been embedded with a strong sense of Asian values and behaviours that work well in this part of the world. But as we start to expand our influence globally, work with more diverse groups of people, and manage more complexity and ambiguity, some of our leadership behaviours will need to be adjusted to cater to a broader audience and a more competitive marketplace.

As I try to "punch above my weight" to be a better global leader, I have always nudged myself to:

1. Retain a sense of humility, respect, and empathy, while being able to effectively question and challenge the status quo.

2. Be grounded on execution excellence, while always pushing further out for bolder ideas that can be more competitive, and levelling up for more creative approaches that can lead to better differentiation.

3. Be clear and specific in goals, while encouraging self-sufficiency and different approaches in achieving these goals, to allow for continuous improvement and draw out valuable learnings from the enterprise.

4. Not try and "save face", but be open to standing corrected, be open to managed risk, and learn quickly from failure.

We have a great foundation that we can build on if we just take a chance and stretch ourselves a bit more!

CHAPTER 2

Subvert the Inferiority Complex

"The most common way people give up power
is by thinking they don't have any."
ALICE WALKER

SINCE TRADE ROUTES from the West were established to the Indian subcontinent and Southeast Asia in the 15th century, European-style colonial empires and imperialism operated in Asia in one form or another throughout a prolonged span of six centuries. Directly and indirectly, Asia was greatly influenced by Western political structures, education, industrialisation, innovation, commerce, and culture over the course of this era. In colonial societies such as Singapore in the 19th and 20th centuries, top positions in government and business were dominated by members of the colonial set; they were seen as more educated, skilled, and cultured than we were. An innate deference to Western leaders continues till today. How many times have you seen your Asian counterparts treat their Western colleagues or bosses with a lighter touch and much more deference than they would their Asian ones?

But much time has passed, and Asians have become more educated, globally exposed, and more experienced as economies have developed. We must be aware that we are very much on par with our Western counterparts when we go head-to-head in business and must now build up the confidence to exert our leadership and influence – tempered, of course, with our natural tendency towards humility and in a style that is comfortable for us.

When the mayor of Taipei, Ko Wen-je, first took office, he made a controversial statement in an interview with *Foreign Policy*, stating that, in reference to countries like Singapore, "the longer the colonisation, the more advanced a place is".[4] And he is not alone in the belief that colonisation has brought positive effects that include, mainly, economic prosperity.

But using the Singapore example, I thought it worth mentioning that Lee Kuan Yew – the nation's founding Prime Minister – championed the concept of "Asian values" as a bulwark against the Western cultural hegemony spreading across the world. What is also interesting to note is that, while Asian values were promoted, it did not mean that anything Western was tossed away.[5] Rather, anything that was practical and useful was assimilated into the nation-building project, as is the pragmatic Singaporean way. And that is the spirit I want to highlight in this chapter.

Dealing With Insecurities

As mentioned earlier, my family moved to the U.S. when I was a teen. Adjusting to life overseas was difficult, but it gave me an opportunity very early in my life to work out where I would fit in and how to be my own person in a majority Western environment. Would I try desperately to blend in, giving up my Asian identity and taking on a purely Western persona? Or would I be defiant, take a closed approach and become even more Asian by associating only with Asians? Within the context of adolescent growing pains and the travails of high school and university, the answer was a confusing mix of yes and yes!

In the world of business, you will be able to see some of these identity-defining behaviours increasingly manifest themselves as more Asians enter the multinational business arena. For example, it is not uncommon to see Asians always congregating together at global meetings, no matter their individual nationality.

As for me, it was not till much later that I settled and became comfortable in my own skin. Those formative years allowed me to morph into various representations of myself and allowed me to determine which identities represented a confident me, and which were just masks I put on to pander to other people.

Despite Asians being a minority in a usually Western-dominated MNC environment, and the idea that colonisation demonstrated the superiority of the West, people are pretty much all the same. It is very important for Asians to cross this mental hurdle. Every single person, no matter their race or nationality, has the same professional insecurities, and the same need to fit in. Above all, most people tend to view each other equally.

What is critical is to gain the trust and respect of your peers through your own words and actions, not the colour of your skin, so that you can have the confidence to stand on equal footing with them. You do have the same right to have your voice heard, and you are entitled to be their superior if you are qualified for the job. In my experience, though, it does take practice to overcome this mental hurdle – at least it did for me.

My first Western direct report was a seasoned Managing Director, an Australian running the South Korean arm when I assumed regional responsibilities as a Regional Manager taking care of Singapore, Malaysia, Taiwan, and South Korea. Taiwan was being run by a long-time Taiwanese gentleman. I found it more natural and easier to work with my Taiwanese MD. I suppose he was more accepting and there was also that due respect accorded to each other as our relationship and communication was rooted in better understanding, familiarity and empathy given our similar cultural backgrounds.

The Australian, on the other hand, was very headstrong and he clearly had done well with the business there. He was direct and rather set in his ways. We were both trying to find our feet together in terms of how we managed the relationship. It was a very uncomfortable time for me as he was significantly older than I was, more experienced in the business than I was, and was also figuring out in his own way how to deal with having a non-Western boss for the first time.

My insecurities played havoc. But by persevering, and with the help of time and clear one-on-one communication and alignment, we managed to get into a natural cadence in our working relationship based on accountability and mutual respect. It was not the most chummy relationship, but it was a professional one.

Look Beyond the Surface

Certainly, I will admit that I did adopt a more measured management style for my Australian colleague. There were times when we disagreed, and I would defer to some of his judgement. I had to be wary that egos weren't at play and that "saving face" didn't factor in, and that it was all about getting the job done, and achieving the best outcomes for the business. Sometimes you simply must adjust your management style and the way in which you interact with your colleagues. Assuming there is a good level of competency and similar values, it's really their job to take the lead, and yours to guide.

To get the results you need without antagonising or disrespecting your people – that is the goal. I learnt to step back and think about the right style to approach others from this experience. Where can I add value, and how do I continue to get results regardless of our business relationship? No matter the race or nationality, people look at each other as contributing colleagues to the same cause at the end of the day.

I have since learnt that all these insecurities were very much in my mind. If you exude the right qualities as a leader, are competent, take care of your people, and always remain fair, most people will naturally follow you. But if you are indeed all those things, and issues remain, then recognise that the problem may not necessarily lie with you.

It takes time and practice to gain confidence in leading colleagues of other nationalities, so the earlier you get exposed to this, the better you will get at it. Eventually you will be able to extend the same support and fair and confident leadership to all.

I have since had numerous colleagues of different nationalities and races report to me and have partnered with many Western colleagues at the same senior level. It's become a natural part of my course of work, and since shedding this inferiority complex, the greater diversity I now experience in thought, approaches and even pushback from my global set of colleagues has in turn made me a better partner and leader.

ASIAN LEADERSHIP LEARNING
Taking the Time to Be a Leader Amongst Leaders
Ng Tian Chong, MD, Greater Asia, Hewlett-Packard

I first met Ng Tian Chong when I was a young officer cadet in the Singapore Armed Forces. He was serving his national service as an officer trainer (only the best of the best became trainers), and was a prime example of an outstanding leader to all of us. The strong validation of this was Tian Chong winning the prestigious Sword of Honour among his cohort of officers. I remember him as a firm and fair officer who had high standards while at the same time being very generous in sharing his knowledge, and in providing timely encouragement throughout the very challenging Officer Cadet Course.

Personally, I experienced an act of his generosity that I haven't forgotten. I was on track to break the longstanding record time for the Standard Obstacle Course. All my practice runs indicated that I could do it. Tian Chong had in the previous year put up one of the fastest times on the course and set a high benchmark. On the day of the run, I went about my paces and was all set in my mind to achieve the record. Unfortunately, when I got to the rope climb section, I slipped all the way down and had to redo the obstacle, wasting a lot of precious time. My heart dropped as I thought I had lost my opportunity. After exerting much more energy to make up for time and navigating the rest of the obstacles, I got onto the last leg of the course, which was a long sprint to the finish line. I felt my energy depleted after trying to make up for time and thought the record was gone. To my surprise, I heard a blast of encouragement and a solid figure sprinting up by my side, egging and pushing me along. It was Tian Chong. Because of him pacing me and telling me (yelling!) that I could still make it, my second wind kicked in and I managed to break the record in full measure!

This is typical of Tian Chong and his leadership approach. He is laser-focused on what he wants to achieve personally, but has also always brought people along with him and helped set them on their own paths to success.

At the time this book is written, Tian Chong leads the Asia-Pacific region for Hewlett-Packard (HP), and is one of the highest-ranking Asians within the enterprise. He is an example of a confident Asian leader who has always believed in his abilities (and has backed this up with performance), has been deliberate and planful of his career, and champions the notion that Asians can and must have a voice on the global business stage.

In trying to understand where this personal confidence stems from and how he has achieved this level of success, his lifelong practices serve as strong guides for us to draw upon.

1. Continuous Learning

Tian Chong is a veteran in HP, having served more than 30 years. Despite being in one company throughout his career, he has made it a point to ensure thoughtful job rotation so he is able to learn all aspects of the business and form a solid foundation and knowledge base. He has been exposed to the myriad of HP's product lines, operated on both the solutions and sales ends of the spectrum, and has worked locally while also taking on multiple regional roles. All this has helped him form a broad base of knowledge and rounded perspective in effectively managing the dynamics of the business, organisation and customers.

While fully engaged in his day job, Tian Chong continued his voluntary service with the Singapore Armed Forces for 32 years and recently completed his service with the pinnacle roles of Division Chief of Staff (Div Hub) and Brigade Commander, overseeing the complexity of building the organisation, capability and executing complex field operations. This dual role at HP and the army has served Tian Chong well in the cross-pollination of learning and experience. When he is faced with complex issues at work, he draws experience from his army operations and how they deal with multifaceted issues and scenarios to overcome them. And when he is faced with the pressure of planning and executing real-time army ops, he similarly draws from his HP work and organisation knowledge to apply them to each scenario for an even more effective outcome.

The attitude of learning, drawing experiences, and re-applying knowledge serves as a great learning example for us to adopt as we strive for continuous learning and career progression. The solid knowledge foundation, together with broadened experience, has helped Tian Chong develop confidence in his management ability to face all scenarios and to lead a diverse group of people.

2. Networking: Expanding Your Circle of Influence

Networking – upwards, downwards and across the organisation – is something that Tian Chong is a big believer in. And this is not just about getting ahead. Asians have a tendency to think that as we move away from our safe and common group – and make the effort to reach out to organisation leaders, lean on stakeholders for support, have social mixes outside of our circle of influence – that others in the group might see this as "brown-nosing". Far from it. As Tian Chong explains, it is important to network internally and externally to understand and gather a wide range of perspectives, which subsequently helps in sharpening your overall work and approach. It's a great way to receive informal feedback, guidance, and different viewpoints. It also builds confidence for you to interact with people of all levels and backgrounds, and enables more people in the organisation to know you and your personal brand.

Other ways to expand one's network include taking on overseas assignments as well as board/directorship roles. Tian Chong makes the effort and feels fortunate to have been given the opportunity to take on board roles and non-executive director positions in regional and global companies, as well as with startups. This allows him to get the exposure he needs to support and work with leaders sitting in various geographies and dealing with specific market and global issues. The exposure allows him again to gain confidence in dealing with broader issues and to guide leaders from various backgrounds and nationalities. This has also helped him build the confidence to stand his ground when needed, voice his opinions and share his experiences – and have the belief that they matter! In this way, Tian Chong is also laying his personal groundwork for future larger roles within the enterprise.

3. Embracing Diversity

Part of a leader's success revolves around building great organisations and teams. The secret sauce to this success lies in embracing and managing diverse characters and thoughts. We talked earlier in this chapter about how the first action of managing senior leaders of other nationalities can be daunting. Tian Chong doesn't quite see it that way. The challenge he has experienced in this area doesn't necessarily fall within race or nationality, but more in managing any senior leader with an opposing, and especially, strong and forceful character. These leaders tend to exude self-confidence, deep experience and understanding of their business and marketplace, and many a time offer opposing or differing views. The mark of great leadership is to embrace these diverse points of view, while also building trusted relationships, so that better solutions emerge, and a bridge for alignment is achieved.

Again, having confidence and a strong knowledge foundation allows you to stand your ground where it makes sense, but also helps you recognise when others have more elegant solutions which you should adopt. All this takes experience and practice, and the earlier you gather your confidence, the sooner you will be able to manage diverse thoughts and strong characters effectively. Start the practice now!

As the younger generation becomes ever more confident in their skin to speak out and voice their opinions, the leaders of the future must see themselves as *connectors* – seeking out great ideas, best practices, divergent points of view, and bringing all these organically together to harmonise into better ideas and a greater good! In Tian Chong's words, it was enough for managers of yesterday to be great symphony conductors and get everyone playing to the same tune, but the leaders of tomorrow must be more like jazz conductors, letting the players find their own rhythm and beat, yet at the same time harmonising to create beautiful music together.

Finally, Tian Chong offers that MNCs should not just adopt a one-size-fits-all Western view towards Asia but try and understand what the real measure of success of Asian-based businesses should be, based on the local context. If success is measured in consideration of Asian terms, and by the effectiveness in navigating Asian markets, there would be much less sense of Asian leaders feeling inferior. The yardstick should be one that allows the Asian leader to freely express his or her latent leadership skills in a way that is appropriate and effective for the local marketplace.

One Last Point... Being an Introvert is No Excuse

A lot has been written recently about the mistaken view of introverts, and how they should be understood and managed. I am naturally an introvert. I enjoy my personal time alone and am not the best at socialising, small talk, or making new acquaintances. I do not necessarily thrive in the limelight. According to one of my personality assessments, I am keen on details and analysis, doing things by the book, and not encouraged to manage big teams!

Doesn't that sound quite fitting for the Asian stereotype? Now, contrast this to my position in China driving a big vision; growing and managing a huge organisation; inspiring people to their full potential; dealing with a multitude of business, media, and government stakeholders; and refining strategy in a twisting and turning VUCA environment. Within a multinational context, Asians tend to be less assertive. While this is not the definition of an introvert, the more salient point is that we must find our own way that does not deviate from our natural self to step up, get into the game, to exert influence, to be heard, and ultimately, to earn a place at the leadership table.

I have always recognised myself as someone with an average start in the business world. But I have worked at being observant, self-aware, empathetic, creative, willing to change, and able to see things from someone else's perspective. I started at ground zero and navigated my way to being a top Asian leader within an MNC. If I can do it, you can too.

PART 2

Developing Your Leadership Voice

CHAPTER 3

Taking on the Leadership Mantle

"It took me quite a long time to develop a voice,
and now that I have it, I am not going to be silent."
MADELEINE ALBRIGHT

AS WE PROGRESS FROM executive and managerial roles to more senior leadership positions, we sometimes forget in our traditional Asian hierarchical psyche that we are the ones now making the decisions, we are the ones setting the agenda versus just taking direction and executing it. We forget that we must look beyond the frenzy of achieving business results and KPIs to also bring our teams along with the agenda and inspire our organisation towards our vision. We forget that our circle of influence and our list of stakeholders have expanded, which means we now must approach issues from a much broader and strategic perspective. We sometimes forget our new position and the corresponding power shift, and wait for direction and permission to make bold moves – but who are we waiting for? We *are* it!

The desire to be promoted and move up in position seems all well and good, but the shock to the system given your new set of responsibilities and accountability can sometimes be overwhelming. In your senior leadership role, you are no longer a follower or a doer. You are setting the agenda, setting the pace, setting the direction. Everyone in the organisation above and below your rank is now looking to you. This paradigm shift comes less easy to Asians who are used to working in a "tell me and I will get it done" environment.

So, being aware of this shift early is important for taking the leadership initiative at the start of your appointment. Being the leader means you need to act like it, from day one. No more passive leadership – you must step up and drive the agenda or someone (in the worst case, your boss) will drive the agenda for you. Understand that in your senior position, your circle of influence has expanded, and over time you will grow in confidence in exerting more influence through your stakeholders and network.

As business leaders, we "live and die" by the vision and direction we take the company on, and by the eventual results that are achieved at the pace we put the business on. The one lens I always keep in mind as I continually review the robustness and aggressiveness of my plan is this: If someone else were to take over my role today, would she be able to change the trajectory of the business more positively than I'm doing now? If the answer is yes, then what am I currently not doing that is required of me? How do I muster up the courage and confidence to do better?

First Things First: Earn Your Place at the Table

I was a young manager when I first joined McDonald's and I did find it difficult as I was thrust into leading colleagues who were older and had more tenure and experience. When

I was first promoted as Director of Operations, all my fellow directors were 20-year veterans. They were clearly giving me the once-over when I came onboard the team.

I felt I had to prove myself to them. I could not get a voice on the table from the start because all of them were so experienced. They were robust in the conversations, and before I could even think about what I wanted to say, I was already talked over. And so I felt that I had to change my style so that I too could be part of the conversation. That experience pushed me to think about how best I could muscle into an already established group.

How do I be a part of that? First, I had to be prepared for every meeting instead of waiting till the last minute to put my hand up whilst a conversation was already well under way. Second, and perhaps most importantly, I had to have confidence in what I wanted to say. Maybe the combined experience level of the people in the room intimidated me. So what? I knew and understood that my words had value, so I knew I had the right to share them.

If you do not engage, why are you at the leadership table? Or to put it in another way, if you want more responsibility and if you want to take on broader leadership roles, you must actively participate and contribute ideas. You must be a part of all the conversations, both formal and informal. You need to be in the thick of it, test your words in the marketplace of ideas. As conversations and discussions flow at a fast and furious pace, nobody will wait for you to process what is going on or to gather your thoughts. If you do not jump in, the train will pass you by.

And this is an attitude that you must bring with you no matter the setting. There have been a few organisation settings across multiple time periods that significantly threw me off-balance and showcased how inadequate I was at skilfully engaging in the conversation. This was especially so when I faced new environments and groupings with a whole other set of participants with much more seniority and experience. I was comfortable in my own circle of influence but began losing confidence as my voice was thrown into foreign environments or discussing topics outside my comfort zone.

In those early years, I was not adept at thinking on my feet, and I did not have the broader depth of knowledge to carry out conversations over many topics, formal or informal. When I was working in Singapore Airlines, one of the informal clubs that new administrative officers were encouraged to attend was Toastmasters. It offered a great social and informal environment for younger recruits to hone their speaking and presentation skills – skills that could be applied in the work environment. I realised then that I was just not good at speaking off the cuff; not great at thinking on my feet; and I was also not well-read enough to discuss a myriad of topics. I could not even coherently present a topic over a dismal five to ten minutes.

So I learnt. I brushed up on my knowledge, and I polished my conversational and public speaking skills at these gatherings. The more you push yourself out of your comfort zone and work on these skills, what may seem unnatural at first to you will soon be second nature, no matter how much of an introvert you are. To get your place at the table, you must earn it.

It is especially important these days that when social media and interactive news just conjure up snappy headlines, we must make the conscientious effort to go beyond the surface and understand the underlying issues that matter to your business or organisation and not leave this understanding just at a superficial level. We need to have a broad perspective and understanding of issues to offer a better assessment of any given situation.

I believe I also fall into the typical Asian camp of being gun-shy when it comes to asking questions or participating in discussions, for fear that the questions might be silly, or the contribution might not add any value. So better to stay silent than sounding stupid, or worse still, drawing attention to you because of that!

When I attended my first Global Senior Leadership meeting among the top executives of McDonald's to discuss and debate the strategic directions that would guide the company, I so wanted to be able to contribute and add perspective. Being a key representative from Asia, I felt I could offer a different point of view that would enrich the diversity of global ideas. Perhaps due to lack of confidence, and the insecurity of not wanting to look silly, I sat through the meeting doe-eyed and with little participation, while the rest of my global colleagues clawed to engage. I felt small and dejected after those rounds of meetings and chided myself for not being worthy of being part of the global leadership team if I couldn't engage and contribute.

Over the next few annual meetings, I decided to do better. Even if my comments or questions were not earth-shattering, I just had to get into the game. For me, preparation was key, and I committed to providing feedback, offering comments, or asking questions on as many occasions as it made sense. There were times when my participation was received with enthusiasm, and there were times when my comments fell flat and faded away into the quiet. Nevertheless, I became an active and thoughtful participant over time. Gaining confidence as a member of the team and actively practising how to participate in meetings made engagement become more natural. There is a well-known Chinese saying: "He who asks a question is a fool for five minutes; he who does not remains a fool forever."

As I reflect on those episodes and now as I facilitate my own leadership and strategy meetings, I understand how facing an audience that offers nothing but deafening silence – when any kind of feedback is sought after – can be extremely frustrating. Is no one responding to what I am saying, doesn't anyone have any comments, are there no questions or challenges to the plan? Does anybody care at all? These are all reasons why meetings (productive ones at least) are held: to evoke a response from the team, to get input to make the plans more robust. When I now canvas the audience and observe especially those who don't participate, I do wonder if they are at all engaged, and if they are with the programme…. This is an impression of you that you surely don't want to leave your stakeholders with.

I know we can't change everyone's behaviour overnight. So I want to offer some tips for those of us that lead Asian teams who exhibit these passive traits in meetings, or who you need to draw out to provide open feedback. These are methods that I have used to give them the best chance to participate successfully and confidently:

1. Provide any pre-reads for the meeting to allow the participants to digest the material and prepare – remember that not everyone is good at thinking on their feet.

2. Be explicit in telling the participants ahead of time that you will be asking for feedback, comments or clarifications, and you expect all to participate. This sounds obvious, but many a time, the general audience looks to the one or two eager contributors to take care of the Q&A sessions. Be sure they know that everyone is fair game to be picked on to participate.

3. Start your meetings on a light note to remove any tension in the air. I have made it a practice to start most of my key meetings with a "fun start" by appointing in rotation one of the participants to offer 5–10 minutes of levity, be it puzzles, jokes, videos, sharing, etc., to break the ice and create an atmosphere for more free-flowing discussion.

4. Make it a habit to draw out questions, and make the effort to go around the room to solicit feedback if none is forthcoming.

5. When you are asking for feedback and no one raises their hands, persist in the silence and human nature will naturally want to break that uncomfortable silence with a response!

As a side note, we must recognise that the whole Covid-19 work-from-home mode might have set us back a bit in the area of "showing up". In the new era of virtual meetings and Zoom calls, many of our local talent might have unconsciously taken the easier route of hanging back and staying in the background in their communication and engagement routines. The virtual environment, while sometimes more productive, has also allowed for video screen-offs, and less time for discussion, questions and comments given the set-meeting-time limitations. As we get back into our more usual routines of interaction post-Covid, let's be sure to encourage the return to active and present participation.

Be a Steward of the Business

One of the biggest differences in how we approach our roles as leaders in the East vis-à-vis the West is the way we manage the set deliverables versus how we dynamically give shape to the business, brand and organisation. As we aspire to the top leadership roles, we must be cognisant that there are significantly more dimensions and layers of issues when leading an enterprise at a higher level. There is also always a whole set of competing priorities that must be constantly juggled and dynamically sequenced.

In Asia, the tendency is for leaders to take the narrow and more structured lane of achieving the KPIs set out for them. All that is well and good for one's performance rating, and for any organisation to stay focused. It's important that there is always a clear plan and a consistent view of targets that can be aligned through the enterprise so that proper execution can take place.

Where we need to elevate our thinking as leaders of the enterprise, however, is beyond KPIs and targets. We should aspire to think of ourselves as *stewards of the business* – always meeting our necessary short-term goals, but at the same time flexing in and out of the key issues and megatrends to be able to dynamically shape the organisation towards a longer-term vision.

In an article in the *New York Times*, Steven Nardizzi, CEO of the Wounded Warrior Project, provides his definition of what it means to be a steward of the business: "Stewards are institutional leaders. They act as responsible caretakers for organizations, large and small, which seek to improve and expand. For stewards, the pressures of short-term performance, financial or otherwise, threaten to compromise long-term goals, and the challenge for institutional stewards is to navigate these external pressures. Faced with competing responsibilities, stewards must remain committed to their organization's long-term mission through short-term strategies that stay faithful to the organization's core values."[6]

A steward of the business is the gatekeeper of a strong and inspiring vision. She must have the ability to frame up the business with robust strategies that people can immediately see and trust. People need to have confidence in the values underlying those strategies as that will drive the business forward.

A steward of the business focuses not only on just getting results; she is also cognisant of the fact that she needs to develop the organisation into a thriving one filled with good talent. That is where good culture in an organisation comes into play. Places like that have people who are clear about what they need to do, in relation to their individual roles within the organisation. Those who merely run the business do not think about the overall health of the organisation because they are only focused on getting the results.

Stewardship also comes with deft management of stakeholders. Stewards must have the ability to communicate clearly the 360-degree view of what's going on with the business. Managing risks is part of this because while executing a plan we must also understand the risks around us and be able to communicate that effectively to the stakeholders.

ASIAN LEADERSHIP LEARNING
Bridging Cultures, Leading with Purpose
Belinda Wong, Chairman, Starbucks China

I have keenly followed Belinda's career for many years as we coincidentally seem to have taken very similar paths. Both of us started as marketers, moved on to Managing Director roles (and at the same time in Singapore in 2004, when she was MD of Starbucks there) and subsequently took on the top leadership roles in China.

Under Belinda's leadership as CEO of Starbucks China, the business has grown by leaps and bounds and has become the second-largest contributor to the global enterprise on the back of world-class operations and stellar results. Howard Schultz, the founder of Starbucks, has always predicted the inevitability of China one day surpassing the U.S. to become the leading business unit globally. This is a show of unmatched confidence and a solid recognition of Belinda and her team's abilities.

While working in China, I saw first-hand how Starbucks

has crafted a locally relevant coffee proposition for the Chinese consumer (in a market where traditional Chinese tea dominates), elevated the brand to be one that is aspirational, and built world-class cafés at a rapid pace, with thoughtful customer experience and design at each point of sale. What I was most impressed with, however, was how they championed the well-being of their partners (barista teams) by putting in place progressive and innovative people policies that have set the benchmark in the industry. Belinda has been at the helm in China for more than 11 years and now serves as the Chairperson of Starbucks China.

While Belinda may now appear well-polished in her role, she too has had to grapple with a lot of the common Asian shortcomings and opportunities that we have been exploring in this book. In discussing how she has successfully navigated the China business as part of a global enterprise all this while – and what she has had to master to take on the leadership mantle and be a steward of her business – Belinda points to four key learnings:

1. Building Leadership Presence

Throughout her career, Belinda has had to build on her confidence and develop her leadership impact as she moved up the company ranks. She would be the first to say that her stage presence was somewhat lacking in the earlier part of her career. Like many of us, Belinda was more comfortable with blending into the background when the time came for vocal participation. Her insecurities lay in her discomfort with public speaking and not having the confidence and courage to speak her mind when it was called for. As she moved up the ranks, Belinda came to the realisation that this leadership posture would not cut it. She needed to quickly learn how to make her voice heard, and with impact! Her employees were all looking to her for clear and inspired direction, her global stakeholders were seeking her out to demystify local complexities with articulate insight that only she could offer, and she had to present confidently laid-out plans that would call for approval and resources.

Practice makes perfect, and with the encouragement and allowance that her people and stakeholders afforded her because of her genuine, authentic and visionary approach, Belinda soon gained the confidence to take a firm hold of her leadership role. She would reciprocate this trust throughout her career by striving to be a grounded servant leader. She would lead from the front, continue with her practice of honing her presence for impact, with the goal of lifting everyone to capture the opportunities in front of them.

With regard to speaking and showing up, Belinda notes an intrinsic difference between the Asian attitude and Western practice. Our Western colleagues have been brought up to have more self-confidence and belief that speaking up and voicing opinions are common rights. In global sessions, you can well observe their robust participation and engagement. In Asia, we have been brought up with the practice that you should speak only when spoken to. We feel that we also need to earn the right to speak up – so unless we have some significant value to add, best that we just stay silent and not risk looking silly. Softer participation modes like offering comments, validating what has been said, reflecting on topics, etc., all seem rather frivolous and unnecessary. Clearly, this is a mistaken point of view, and we must learn to contribute to the ongoing discourse constructively.

2. Self-Reflection and Self-Improvement

Belinda's biggest critic is herself. She has a keen drive for excellence and always wanting to do better – for the business and for her personal development. And she is willing to put in the hard work to improve. Whenever something doesn't quite pan out the way she thinks it should have, Belinda would take a step back, process the learnings and reflect on what could have been done better, or how she could have handled the situation differently. Her best learnings have come from her failures. Over the course of her career, she has mastered the skill of self-reflection, which has led her to find the right balance between difficult and competing leadership behaviours, for example:

- Being nurturing vs Being objective in managing people.

- Being diplomatic vs Being candid in coaching her team.

- Driving hard vs Bringing people along when change is required.

By taking the time to reflect on both her leadership shortfalls and successes – drawing not only from quantitative results but also from other qualitative feedback channels – Belinda has been able over time to hone her leadership approaches to be nimble and adaptive to any situation that comes her way. Her standard of measure would be: Given a similar situation the second or third time round, would she handle it with a more effective approach and with a better outcome? If the answer is yes, the time taken for self-reflection would have been meaningful, the discipline to adapt would have been worthwhile, leading to a better outcome for all, and personally shaping her into a more trusted and effective leader.

3. Building a Bridge of Trust

Belinda believes that for an Asian leader to be a true steward of the business in a multinational organisation, she needs to be an effective gateway of communication and understanding between the local market and global stakeholders. And with proven results, engagement and transparency, this gateway can develop into a precious "bridge of trust" between the two parties.

When asked to identify what role she plays – as China's CEO – that is most useful for the global enterprise, Belinda believes it is the role of championing local marketplace plans and initiatives that are most effective, while at the same time being the diligent steward of the global brand and its standards. This bridge is easier to build if someone is sent from corporate HQ just to execute a global playbook in the local marketplace. The bridge is not so easy to build when a market strives for more local relevancy and to not just follow the global playbook blindly. This represents our job as Asian leaders as we are sited closer to the field, can better sniff out the opportunities around us, and can sort through more effectively as to what works and what doesn't.

So, we must hone this bridging skillset. We might start on both ends of the bridge with perspectives that are vastly opposite, with different sets of cultural assumptions, with a lack of understanding, and with a shortfall of trust. On her end, Belinda has been conscientiously building this bridge within the Starbucks organisation over the years by:

- Having a strong and viable vision, and then being an articulate storyteller of how these plans will work.

- Translating the needs of the local business to a perspective that the rest of the organisation can understand.

- Being able to share not just the *what* but also the *how* in execution, so that there is comfort that things are done the right way.

- Having the courage to be decisive, and proving the correctness of these decisions over time.

- Taking the lead after alignment is sought, and not having to seek permission at every step; being self-sufficient.

- Being transparent and timely with result or issues, whether good or bad.

- Holding fast to values that are important to the enterprise.

- Championing ideas and talent in assessing the competency of the organisation versus the spotlight that sometimes shines on the inadequacy of language (e.g., English) and presentation.

In her school of hard knocks, Belinda never takes for granted the faith that the enterprise has placed in her to shepherd the business, and continues to take an everyday approach in earning this trust. In doing so, she represents her people and their business aspirations well, while at the same time earning management's trust – a true mark of an effective Asian leader grabbing hold of the leadership mantle and straddling the complexity of a global enterprise!

4. Creating a North Star with Purpose

Belinda believes that as you take on the leadership mantle, it's important to not just drive for business results, but lead the organisation towards a larger common purpose that all stakeholders can believe in and rally around. This is so that all the blood, sweat and tears put in by the employees is not just to earn that last dollar, but that in addition to that, their work contributes to a purpose that everyone believes in and can have a stake in contributing to. This is just how Belinda is wired in her leadership thinking. She came to the realisation early on that the most meaningful purpose of Starbucks' growth in China was the ability to create meaningful jobs and provide development opportunities for her partners (employees). And this subsequently would lead to making a positive impact and lift the local communities where Starbucks operates in.

Career opportunities naturally come with business growth and quick expansion. Every 15 hours, for example, an employee is promoted to a store manager; every week, a store manager is promoted to a district manager; every month, a district manager is promoted to a regional director; and so on. In Belinda's approach, the purpose is the starting point, and she believes – and has successfully proven – that the business naturally falls in place behind a strong and common purpose. Belinda has been able to bring her people along to achieve strong business results and provide a personal stake for each of them to be invested in the journey.

Finally, Belinda points out that the other half of her success has come from having great mentors and leaders from all parts of the organisation supporting her. The ones that she views that have been most effective in partnering her to manage a complex market like China have been:

- Culturally sensitive and aware.

- Courageous in the trust and support of local leaders.

- Helpful in opening doors to the right people and resources within the enterprise.

As organisations look to local leaders to manage their local markets, they should also pay heed to the next level of supervisors so that there can be a right pairing and a right fit, ensuring that the appropriate support can be provided and allowing the bridge of trust to be strengthened.

CHAPTER 4

Heads Up vs Heads Down

"The leader must aim high, see big, judge wisely, thus setting himself apart from the ordinary people who debate in narrow confines."
CHARLES DE GAULLE

I SEE A LOT OF ASIAN executives operating with their "heads down". They diligently focus on their work, they conscientiously execute the tasks given to them, and they doggedly strive to achieve the KPIs set out for them. They may look like they are always frantically busy, jumping from one issue to another, putting out one fire after the other. All that might be well and good, as we do need to resolve day-to-day issues, and we of course also need good soldiers to get things done. Execution prowess is regarded as one of our key strengths!

As we move up the leadership ranks, however, I submit that we need to take on a more "heads up" approach. While getting things done, we need to get our heads out of our turtle shells and observe what is happening around us: to be able to get perspective on what and how we are doing, to be able to identify barriers or roadblocks, to be able to see if the ship continues to sail in the right direction even when conditions change, to be able to sniff out new possibilities.

In today's fast-paced world, it is imperative that you make sure you are taking on a Heads Up approach rather than just a Heads Down approach. Yes, it is tempting to focus only on deadlines and execution, especially when in the thick

91

of it. And especially when you are in a crisis or a fire-fighting situation. But you will quickly lose perspective and not be able to capture the opportunities at the broader level – something a top leader must continue to do during her tenure.

In an article in *Fast Company*, Josh Linkner compares the traits associated with a Heads Down vs Heads Up approach.[7]

Heads Down	Heads Up
Focused on delivery	Focused on possibilities
Tuning out distractions	Embracing new things
Avoiding outside influence	Welcoming outside influence
Execution	Curiosity and awareness
Getting things done	Questioning everything
Right now	The future
What is	What could be
Deadlines	Imagination

This is not a debate on the merits of either posture; rather, it is meant to create awareness that as Asian leaders we need to shift towards more of Heads Up thinking as we move through the leadership ranks. Understand that you now have a system of people below you that can be focused on execution. You need to focus on the broader picture of whether that execution is placed in the right areas and is working.

The Asian model unfortunately tends to focus on that one patrician leader who issues commands to be obeyed. Direction is given and everyone jumps into execution mode as we follow the leader. As we shared in the right-side-up organisation concept, this leadership style must change. You must practise shared leadership, be transparent and clear on your vision and goals, and then allow freedom within the framework for the organisation to execute, and adjust where necessary. You can only adjust if you are not blindly following, but are also monitoring progress, staying abreast of events and circumstances around you, and keeping a finger on the pulse of how your teams are performing – basically keeping your Head Up to get a good perspective on progress.

Perspective and Context

Giving yourself more perspective on any given task is invaluable. We are sometimes focused on the narrow lane of setting goals and then getting down to the business of achieving those targets. In my experience, we sometimes forget to place these goals and actions within the context of a changing landscape. It is rare that we ever operate in a vacuum and don't have competitors close on our heels and anticipating our next moves. We also achieve success through our people, but are we aware if the competency and capability is there to get the job done?

Having perspective leads us then to an informed list of principal points of consideration when attacking a task, to identify risks along the way which we can mitigate, and to determine what capability we need to build to get the job done. It also helps to place us within the environment we are competing in and gives us ideas how we can win in that space. We need to always seek out perspective to help us sort the busy work from the work that matters and can achieve results.

Asian leaders must take more considered time to seek out perspective. Time to read broadly, to see what's in the news that might impact you, to be in-the-know of industry discussions, to have a constant communication channel at all levels of your organisation, to interact with your stakeholders. Asian leaders have to get out more and engage, adopt a Heads Up posture, and get broader perspective as they run their businesses.

Head, Heart and Guts

Another aspect of leading with a Heads Up approach is being able to not just do things right (checking everything off the list safely), but more importantly, to do the right things.

In their book, *Head, Heart and Guts: How the World's Best Companies Develop Complete Leaders*, authors David Dotlich, Peter Cairo and Stephen Rhinesmith reveal the three most important capabilities leaders today must demonstrate: the ability to set strategy, empathise with others, and take risks – all at the same time.[8]

Rely only on using your head to make decisions, and you risk looking theoretical and potentially acting unempathetically. Rely only on your heart, and you may not be able to make the tough decisions that you are sometimes required to. Rely only on your gut and you might be prone to making unforced errors. A senior leader must be able to draw on each capability of head, heart and guts when it comes to decision-making and policy creation.

Fact-based, data-led research will give you the numbers and figures to help you in your strategy and this may take time to compile. The insights they provide must not be thrown away in favour of quick decision-making. Going merely by gut is, realistically, the purview of that exceptional entrepreneur or corporate leader with tons of experience to back it up. Even so, many a gut-made decision has been the folly of experienced leaders. The sweet spot is in enhancing that creative and valuable gut instinct with more data-based insights. It is important for Asian leaders to be aware of this as we often skip the rigour of gathering fact-based insights (takes too long, costs too much), and go for the quick gut call. Imagine all the flaws of Asian leadership coming together in this instance if the gut call is in fact misguided – a whole organisation executing one person's direction, no one challenging that direction along the way, and a lot of Heads Down resources expended executing a plan that is doomed for failure!

When it comes to making heart calls, we must recognise that there are many decisions that logically make sense... but do they take into consideration the people being impacted?

The onset of Covid-19 threw up lots of examples of tough decisions business leaders had to make pitting the financial impact of business continuity (or survival!) with keeping organisations intact. How would decisions be made given the unprecedented pandemic crisis when many businesses faced a hard stop on income?

Like most countries, Singapore made the difficult decision to impose a countrywide lockdown (dubbed a "circuit breaker") at the early stages of the pandemic to protect the vulnerable and unvaccinated population. Classified as an essential business, McDonald's – like most dining establishments – was allowed to continue all non-dine-in operations to continue feeding and serving the community. The crew and managers continuing to work at the frontline were exposed to Covid-19 infections, despite all the possible safety measures and protection that we deployed, and unfortunately, we had seven employees from various outlets who contracted the virus early on. While that number in hindsight now seems relatively small, the zero-Covid strategy adopted by the authorities then prompted them to ask us to stop our market-wide operations to control the spread.

This was a shocking and significant event for us. In all our 40 years of doing business in Singapore, we had never once closed all our restaurants at one go. And now we were to close all of them for three weeks! I remember clearly receiving this news on a Sunday evening. Panic-stricken thoughts filled my mind. How would the business survive without cash from operations? How would we break this news to our people and how would they take it? What would we do with our inventory and perishable produce in the restaurants and our warehouses? How would we manage our suppliers, who rely on our business for their income? How would we communicate the closure to our customers?

Suffice it to say that we survived and even thrived over this long pandemic that continues even at the time this book is being written. I was fortunate to have a fantastic team at the head office and at the restaurants who courageously and doggedly fought through every twist and turn of the pandemic. I will forever be grateful to them, and I will share broader learnings on the crisis in Part 3 of this book. For now, I want to illustrate the decisions made on the people front during this restaurant closure period that best showcase the balanced use of Head, Heart and Guts.

Using our Head, we quickly mapped out our closure plan and the actions we needed to take over the next three weeks in cash financing, supply chain management, restaurant facility management, campaign adjustments and changes, communication plans internally and externally, and keeping all our stakeholders (including our principal, shareholders, authorities, suppliers, partners and employees and their families) updated on a constant and timely basis. We immediately called a Zoom session with all our employees that Sunday evening at 10 p.m.

The one decision we had to clearly make before the call was what was going to happen with employee wages and job security given this dire situation. There would be significant cash burn with no revenue coming in, and the logical – and I daresay, conventional – step would be to impose a pay cut to make up for that loss. But that was not the right decision to make.

What we did instead was far harder, but also had more Heart. The first thing we did on that Sunday night Zoom call was to resolutely assure every single employee that no matter the Covid-19 shutdowns, their jobs were 100% secure and so were their salaries. We asked them to continue to just focus on taking care of their teams and their customers, and we would in turn take care of them.

Of course, by doing this, we would take a financial hit. But taking a broader perspective and a Heads Up look at the situation, it was a mere blip over the 40 years that McDonald's had been in Singapore. The employees had given so much of themselves over those years, and we had clearly been financially successful all that while. We could manage the reduced earnings during this blip, but we certainly could not lose the loyal people who has been working with us for so long. Loyalty is not something that money can buy.

Another difficult people decision we made during the Covid-19 crisis was how to manage our Malaysian employees. In March 2020 and at the peak of the pandemic, Singapore closed its border with Malaysia, impacting innumerable Malaysian workers who would commute across the border to Singapore every day.[9] They had only one day to decide whether they were going to cross over to Singapore and stay for an unknown duration (little did we know at the time that the borders would be shut for over two years). We had about 1,500 Malaysians at that time working with us, and ultimately, about 700 decided to come over to Singapore before the borders shut.

For those 700 or so employees, we placed them in suitable accommodations and provided them with cost-of-living allowances. We kept this up throughout the two years and more of the pandemic and it cost us a sizeable sum. Maybe to anyone else that would seem like a strain on finances and thus not a rational Head decision to make. But to us, it was and is a Heart decision. I still recall seeing our young Malaysian managers and crew leaving their mothers, fathers, wives, husbands and children at the drop of a hat to join us in Singapore. They had faith in us – how could we possibly not repay that faith by taking care of them?

At first glance, this involved a lot of Heart, but dig deeper and you'll see the Guts in this approach. As a leader, you live or die by the sword. When the strategy works well, the CEO gets recognised and remunerated. When it doesn't, the CEO gets fired. Things could have gone really wrong, but we took that gamble because we knew it was the right thing to do. Head, Heart, and Guts all considered.

Throughout the pandemic, our Malaysian staff remained diligent and committed in working with their local counterparts as they continued to serve our customers together. And with the ensuing local manpower crunch that would hit the industry during the pandemic, their presence was a stabilising force in helping the business continue to operate. I continue to view their resilience with admiration.

To take a business on a different trajectory takes Guts, and unfortunately a lot of Asian companies focus on specifically performing and *not failing*. Remember what we discussed about the fear of failure leading us down the path of mediocrity? It is a bit of a death spiral. When you perform just to not fail, you become mediocre, and it keeps dragging you down. But if you stick your neck out a little bit to take on that gutsy chance, you just might shoot all the way up to the top.

CHAPTER 5

Giving Life to Your Strategic Plan

"Without strategy, execution is aimless.
Without execution, strategy is useless."
MORRIS CHANG

WHY AM I TALKING about strategy in the Asian leadership context? Wouldn't the use of strategy just be common practice for leaders in any business? Having operated across multiple Asian organisations, and gathering feedback from leaders in these institutions, a common grouse is that Asian leaders tend to operate more *tactically* and with less *strategic* intent. This might be okay for employees lower in the organisation ranks, but as we scour for top Asian leaders, the adoption of more robust strategic oversight is critical.

Strategy might just be words on a piece of paper for some – something that we craft during planning periods, only to be cast aside as we get on with the daily grind of the business and other urgent priorities. To others, strategy can serve as a powerful guiding force, which, when fully embraced and executed, propels the trajectory of a business and the organisation to success. I don't profess to be an expert on strategy, and there are many other more qualified and competent thought-leaders in this area. But what I can take pride in is how my teams and I have always leaned on, and remained committed to, strategies that had material impact on the business, brought them to life for our stakeholders, and pressed for constant validation to be sure they remained relevant and of value.

As I've mentioned, the action-oriented bias in Asia — with a priority on getting things done rather than spending the time *talking* about getting things done — has set us on a natural path towards busy work. Working hard in Asia often represents a badge of honour; it makes us feel like we have truly earned our keep, and it demonstrates the tangible sacrifice and selflessness that we take upon ourselves to provide for our families and loved ones.

As we lead our teams, how do we organise all this work to be sure that our activity is all worthwhile, and that it progresses the enterprise towards achieving the set-out vision and goals? How can we deliver on plans that are guided by *solid strategy*, and executed with *effective tactics*? We can certainly learn to act and work smarter, and you would think that this approach should be perfect for Asians — the only thing worse than wasting time talking about getting things done is to waste time achieving nothing.

As leaders, part of our job is to craft meaningful strategies to guide all the hard work and effort towards the correct path with common purpose. Some pitfalls I have observed amongst some of my Asian colleagues in thinking about and executing on strategy at a higher level include:

1. Not being able to sift the real strategies (with direction) from the busy work (with no direction).

2. Not making the effort to first identify the real issues or ask more *why* questions. This leads to follow-on strategies that lack insight and are obvious and mediocre right out of the starting gate.

3. Not gaining sufficient leadership or system buy-in to the strategies, leading to soft commitment.

4. Giving up on a powerful strategy at the first misstep on the tactical level – the execution might have taken a wrong turn, but it doesn't mean that the strategy is incorrect.

5. Launching and leaving, i.e. deploying a strategy with a bang, but then quickly turning to other priorities, leaving the energy of the organisation around it to fizzle out.

To that end, let me share a few thoughts and case studies on what we can to do to craft better strategies, bring them to life, and sustain them for the long-haul.

Surfacing Relevant, Compelling Strategies

Strategy is about the allocation of the organisation's time, money and resources. The critical job for senior leaders then is to choose and prioritise the precise strategies that can reap the biggest benefit for the business, the stakeholders, and the organisation. Some of these choices can be difficult to make, and I would submit that the more robust, competitive and differentiated strategies take a more persistent and longer path to achieve. If the strategy or choice we make is easy, then it should be similarly easy for every competitor, and they would eventually be able to "eat our lunch". A good strategy creates a moat around your castle, keeping your competitors at bay – at least for a while.

A strategy that is bold, robust and competitive might sometimes seem insurmountable to the internal organisation, by its very nature of being difficult or far-reaching. So you can imagine that there will be quite a bit of buy-in needed, good communication on not just the *what* but also the *why* of the cause, and periods of persistence when roadblocks are encountered. A strategy that takes iteration and time should not be allowed to suffer the "launch and leave" syndrome – a nice idea at the beginning, but one that loses steam after some setbacks or with no leadership commitment to persist over the long run. When things get difficult, human nature tends to lead us down the easier path and move us from a strong and robust strategy to... mediocrity.

Strive to Be More Creative

Anita Roddick, founder of the Body Shop, espoused: "Be creative. Be anything but mediocre!"

Asians tend to adopt a herd mentality and to go with the flow when it comes to ideation. There is less appetite to be contrarian, especially when the majority has decided to move down a certain direction. A senior leader must have the courage to challenge the status quo against all odds and push for a more worthy solution or a more creative and differentiated approach.

Our herd mentality often leads us to the lowest common denominator – everybody is doing it and so we should too. This is the "copy mentality" that leads to mediocrity. This is also the stigma Asians are unfortunately stuck with, that we are good at copying and generating copycat or fake items, all for a quick buck. This hit-and-run tactical approach might generate some small change, but it obviously has no legs or foundation to stand on as a sustainable venture. There are times when it might make sense for us to ride on the momentum of a certain trend, but we should also always strive to act like a leadership brand and business and set the pace for the industry.

If we look at Apple and Foxconn as examples, we see two clearly outstanding and winning businesses. It is quite obvious that the company that generates the significantly higher value is Apple. Apple is built on ideation, design and innovation, and demands a more creative mandate that differentiates itself from its competitors. And this differentiated advantage has allowed it to enjoy success over a sustained period. Foxconn is also a thriving business, a multinational contract manufacturer that produces electronic products for numerous leading global brands in the technology space. It is one of the largest employers worldwide. By value comparison, the company that generates ideas (and that can also execute), Apple, has a market cap of US$2.5 trillion, and the company that contract-manufactures for them, Foxconn, has a market cap of US$88 billion. While different in magnitude, these are both valuations that any company board would die for. And this is certainly not about pitting one great organisation against the other, but to generate more of an aspiration for Asian leaders and companies to move up the value chain with more innovation, creativity and differentiation. We need to move from our mediocre copy mentality and up the value chain to differentiated and creative solutions.

If an idea or strategy is mundane, if it does not get me excited, I will take a step back and think through it again. After all, if I'm not excited with it, how can I possibly get my organisation energised behind it? The strategy could be very logical and very rational, but if it is not a creative and differentiated vision for us all, it is still not going to be a solid strategy to implement. How could we change it to be more inspiring and allow us to win? Can we create something that we can really be excited about? If so, then it will be ready to be shared with everyone. You need to find more creative solutions to those issues.

When formulating our strategies, we go about it in a few phases. In the first phase, we take a step back and identify the key issues facing the business, size up current and new marketplace opportunities, and have a longer-term understanding of the emerging megatrends. This is more of a self-reflection and diagnostic phase to surface up all the challenges and opportunities.

In the second phase, we use this information and set our longer-term vision (three to five years), outlining the broad strategic pillars that will get us there. As a lens, we always ask ourselves if this vision that we set is inspiring, and if it is worthy of a market leader. Have we used the facts and thought creatively enough about the plan such that our strategies are robust and invigorating? We overlay ideas on how we can win:

- How do we win in this type of environment?
- How do we win in terms of results?
- How do we win our consumers' hearts?
- How do we win this part of the brand?
- How do we win over this section of the community?

In the last phase, we take these thoughts into an annual one-year plan where budgets are set and capital expenditures given, and where near-in execution is planned for. We operationalise the plan throughout the organisation so that every employee understands the long-term bigger picture but also knows what needs to be executed in the coming year, all of which adds to the layering of that vision wall.

In every phase of this planning process, we socialise the thoughts, directions and ideas to see what sticks with our stakeholders and what seems to fall flat. Being collaborative in the approach to planning and generating the strategies based on insight, but also on creative and differentiated approaches, separates a great plan from a merely good one. You must figure out if what you are going to do is good enough or exciting enough. We do not want run-of-the-mill things that everybody else is doing. That is not leadership, that is just following everybody else.

Name That Strategy

There are times that we knowingly or unwittingly hit on an initiative that works, is successful, and we achieve good results. How do we capture and put a name to the action we just undertook? How do we draw learnings from it? How do we have a common language so that we can replicate success and share what we did so that others in the system can benefit from it? It is difficult to differentiate that winning formula from mere busy work if you do not define it. And it is even harder to test it.

Once the strategic choices are made, a critical first step to socialising this to a larger audience is to put a name to the strategy – one that is precise, clear and simple for your organisation and stakeholders to understand. Hopefully, one that also inspires and endures through the life of the strategy. During my tenure at McDonald's, whenever we put out a longer-term strategy, we also tried to put a name to it.

Not Just McDonald's, But *Singapore's* McDonald's

When I took over the McDonald's business in Singapore the second time round at the end of 2016 – and this time as an equity partner and licensee – the business was in a bit of a stalemate. McDonald's had been in Singapore for 38 years at the time, was the clear market leader in the quick-service restaurant category, and had widely distributed retail presence and a strong brand reputation.

But like other markets around the world, the food industry was in a period of much disruption: lots of new brands, artisanal cafés and eateries had entered the market; digital transformation in the industry was taking shape; the health and wellness trend was on an uptick; and many new concepts enabled by technology like home delivery, agri-tech and cloud kitchens were fast emerging. In this landscape of wide consumer choice, it was important for us to understand how we could compete, remain relevant, and win.

I had written on a piece of paper the direction I thought the company should take, even before I took over the reins, but I needed to get a sense of the organisation and see where the thinking of our stakeholders (from the restaurant level to our head office teams, and to our principal McDonald's) was at. You can imagine the wide range of opinions, from staying the course and remaining committed to our core business, to becoming more health-and-wellness driven, to catering to

111

the artisanal needs of millennials, and to operating like a digital entity with cloud kitchens and delivery, to name a few.

In formulating strategy, a leader must draw on facts and insights, while keeping an open ear to the diverse opinions within the organisation, and especially those that come from people in the field, who are closest to the customer. With these varied views, it's also important to add your judgment to the mix, drawing on your years of experience (that's part of why you're in the senior position role), and to sift out the real opportunities from the distracting marketplace noise.

In our case, the reality was that while the industry was certainly more competitive, our business at its core was still extremely robust. We had monthly transactions that were more than the population of Singapore – that can't be a sign of weak business at all. So why should we want to try and compete with and be like an artisanal one-store concept? Shouldn't we draw on our strengths and be a better, more modern, more relevant version of ourselves?

I have always believed that when there is traction in any part of the business, we should seek that out and do more of that, as there is already natural consumer affinity. So, we laid out our strengths and areas where we had momentum: we had branches all over Singapore, and particularly in the heartlands; we offered great everyday value and affordable prices; our operational prowess spoke to our consistency, quality and service; and our research showed us that when it came to the family experience and our Western breakfast offering, we were unmatched. Where there is momentum, ride it!

But there were also many things we needed to improve on. We were sales-driven, using promotions and tactics to grow consumer purchases. We weren't balancing that enough with listening to our customers and building the brand and brand trust. This is a common mistake that marketers make. We also needed to modernise our restaurant facilities with new and modern décor, and outfit our customer journey with the relevant technology that our customers were rapidly adopting. We needed to be committed to our global billion-dollar brand offerings like the Big Mac, French Fries and Chicken McNuggets, but we also needed to offer a menu that was relevant to Singapore for comfort, choice and variety. We needed to take care of our key customers – families and kids – and to provide differentiated service and offerings to lead in this category. Many of our restaurants were built decades ago, and with business growth, their operating capacity had become limited. There were lots of opportunities to open new restaurants and penetrate the market even more.

After managing through this strategic exercise with the facts and with the input from all our stakeholders, I pulled out that piece of paper I had written on earlier, and I must say it spoke to me. But more importantly it spoke to all that we needed to do and be. We would be "Not just McDonald's, but Singapore's McDonald's"!

Not only would we offer all the great products and

services that our consumers already love, trust, and have affinity with, we would offer a better version of ourselves in the areas where we would need to transform, and most importantly, we would be even more relevant to the communities and customers we serve, in this instance Singapore and Singaporeans. There is a funny anecdote on local brand relevance that goes like this: A young Singaporean boy is travelling with his mother on a business trip to the U.S. There, he sees the Golden Arches and says to her: "Look, Mum, they even have McDonald's here in the U.S.!"

As a strategy, "Not just McDonald's, but Singapore's McDonald's" set the direction for all aspects of the business: how we would commit to strengthening our core McDonald's operations; how we would think of our menu; how we would think of where to open restaurants (more heartlands to get to the local population); how we needed to stay locally relevant to all consumers (not just millennials, but especially heartland families); how we would commit to giving back to the communities in which we operate; and how we would meet the needs of our ever-changing and increasingly digital-savvy consumers.

As we cascaded this strategy down the organisation and stakeholders, we also wanted to bring this idea to life, so that it offered common purpose, and so that it would have longevity and wouldn't just be a fleeting idea. We framed this into a three-year work plan that would build and strengthen these elements year on year. We picked a milestone of 2019

– our 40th anniversary in Singapore – where we would showcase the culmination of these efforts, celebrate our relationship with Singaporeans, and cement our enduring ties with them.

As a sidenote, when Covid-19 hit us in 2020, this move to be "Singapore's McDonald's", and all the effort that the team made to win back the hearts of local customers, paid dividends as we hunkered down and were able to serve our customers with transformed digital options, having modernised drive-thrus, delivery and takeaway services that customers could use the way they wanted to; having opened up more restaurants in the heartlands, where our customers were as they worked from home or were confined with Covid-19 restrictions; and most importantly, being a brand that was familiar to them and one that they could trust.

ORGANISATION STRATEGY CASE STUDY
A Winning and Caring Team That Proudly Serves

To match the customer-facing strategy of being more relevant to Singaporeans, we had to also be sure that our key stakeholders – our employees – were equally invested in this journey. Naturally, growth means more success for the business, but it also leads to more career opportunities, benefits for all, and fulfilment in jobs that expand in scope and offer new learning and development. How do we then get the entire system energised behind this longer-term business rally cry and gain the conviction of every employee? What would be in it for them?

We framed up an organisation strategy that called on the collective efforts of all of us to be engaged in this plan to win, but at the same time to deliver on this with our core values, and to be sure that everyone benefited from business success. We committed to be a "Winning and Caring Team that Proudly Serves". Each word in the strategy offered a critical imperative for the organisation.

Winning: People obviously want to work for a company that shares the same values as they have and treats people fairly. But I would suggest that everyone also wants to work in a company that is successful and winning. No one wants to work for a losing company. We all want to be part of an organisation that's in the news and in the heat of things; a company that people talk about with admiration; a company that engenders energy and excitement in employees and makes them proud that they are part of this dynamic engine. So, first things first, we all need to do our part to ensure the success of the business.

Caring Team: Executing the business plan is hard enough. Doing it in an environment where we support each other, take care of each other, and understand each other's needs, is a critical support enabler that sustains us in this journey. So, while we drive hard for business results, we need to drive just as hard to take care of our people. With this mandate, we created many underlying tracks of people sub-strategies to ensure that we matched our business initiatives with equally robust people initiatives. We also knew that the pace of the business needed to match the capability and capacity of the organisation. So, we made a commitment to upskill our employees in new and varied areas like business planning, leadership skills, hospitality, and new digitalisation knowledge. We were sensitive to the pace at which we ran. There were times when we had to push hard to take the business initiative and gain momentum, and there were times when we sensed the system was overstretched and we had to consciously release the pressure valve. This sense of understanding and care was much appreciated by the team.

Proudly: There have been many references to the notion of "McJobs", where a career in McDonald's has not been portrayed as an attractive endeavour. I wanted our folks to be proud of working at McDonald's, proud of the services they provide, and proud of their own individual accomplishments. Many employees in McDonald's have had multi-decade careers. Many of them started at the crew level and developed into leadership positions managing million-dollar restaurants and teams. Many have strong success stories of accomplishment and growth. I, too, benefited from the McDonald's system. I started as an Assistant Marketing Manager in Singapore, was given the opportunity to learn the business in all aspects of Restaurant Operations, HR, Supply Chain, Real Estate, Finance, and later held top management positions in Singapore, China, regionally, and now as an owner-operator.

The McDonald's learning and development system is set up such that you can take on your roles part-time and learn all the life-long skills of co-operation, communication and teamwork. You can also make it a career, and there is a systemised training curriculum and progression for you to learn how to run a great restaurant and lead people (all this culminating in a Degree in Hamburgerology from Hamburger University). Many of us have proud stories to tell. We needed to do a better job in changing the perception of McJobs and showcase how truly meaningful our system to develop youth and talent is.

It was also imperative that we act like a leadership brand, lead the industry in fun and exciting market-maker campaigns and lead in contributing to our community in the various efforts that we participate in, like the Ronald McDonald's House Charity and the local community projects that our restaurants contribute to. Being part of a company that has a winning business, one that's a market-maker, and at the same time one that leads with its corporate values is something the organisation can be proud to be part of, and our strategy was to make sure we brought all this to life.

Finally, *Serve*. We are part of the hospitality sector, and we have one of the strongest reputations for offering unrivalled service in the industry. McDonald's founder Ray Kroc and his team established the brand fundamentals of QSC&V – Quality, Service, Cleanliness and Value. Throughout the history of the company, we have all tried to be stewards holding these standards high. But now, we needed to also build on this strength by enhancing our service delivery to be even better and more relevant to changing consumer needs.

We developed a two-prong strategy to do this. One was to shift our renowned step-by-step processed service where there were prescribed ways (six prescribed steps, to be exact) of transacting with the customer to one that was more based on hospitality: engage customers the way that they want to be engaged. This strategy required us to set up and invest in a whole new organisation of Guest Experience Leaders to take better care of our customers, and it also required all of us to shift from our robotic six-step standardised approach to a more flexible "do it your way" hospitality mindset. We adjusted our call to action from QSC&V to QSC&H, adding the H as a shift towards Hospitality as a key pillar.

The second prong of this service approach was to deploy modern and digital technology so that customers would have more control over the way they interact with us, via self-ordering kiosks, digital app ordering, cashless payment options, and even table service. Being the market-maker, we would lead the industry in the mass adoption of these tools. Reinventing our service, we would deploy technology "hardware" while also employing hospitality "heart-ware".

While we culminated this multi-year strategy with our 40th anniversary celebrations for our customers, we also culminated our organisation strategy with a long-term commitment to our people with four legacy anniversary gifts: the gift of learning, the gift of recognition, the gift of celebration and the gift of giving back together. These gifts would reinforce our focus on our people for many years to come.

These business and organisation approaches represented two broad strategies that defined our approach over the three years, and working together with clear focus, it led to turnaround growth, market share gains and year-on-year improvement in people engagement scores. What a solid combination – a winning and caring team that proudly serves Singapore's McDonald's.

Finally, Create a Learning Organisation

One of the traits of good leadership is how we capture the system learnings from these exercises – what worked, what didn't work – and try to bottle that recipe for replicable success, or to learn from mistakes. As Asian leaders, we oftentimes take the results for what they are – celebrate or lament – and move forward "Heads Down" to the next task at hand. We forget to pause and capture the invaluable lessons of the success or shortcomings which we can apply to future endeavours, as well as to create a depository of learning which the enterprise can benefit from.

To do this, we need to take time to step back, evaluate and process what just happened. Of course, all this starts with proper strategic thinking. And as I recommended, putting a name to every strategy will allow you to evaluate each one on its merits and shortcomings.

CHAPTER 6

Win the Present, Build the Future

"The future depends on what we do in the present."
MAHATMA GANDHI

BEFORE I WAS CHOSEN for the CEO role at McDonald's China, I had the opportunity to be assessed and coached by a very experienced and senior talent consultant. One of the watchouts in his assessment of my leadership was that I tended to veer on the side of setting bolder targets and was content to achieve them over the long term. He pointed out that I had to be more conscious of the short-term and give more weight to achieving nearer-term results – and at a more aggressive pace. I agree with this assessment. If you don't generate short-term results and growth, you won't be able to bridge the business to your loftier longer-term goals, and you won't have earned the credibility and the right to more capital expenditure and investment.

But in my experience and interactions, I believe most Asian leaders are already well-tuned to looking for immediate results. This is our main preoccupation. The real area for our development is to be able to achieve that while at the same time being committed to laying out the building blocks for the future. We have discussed in the earlier chapters how good vision and strategy can point to what that future might be and how it can be crafted.

In an increasingly VUCA world, how do we deal with the various crises or exigencies that come our way? These seem like everyday occurrences lately. And how do we not become overwhelmed or distracted from the bigger picture? When things get difficult, we sometimes abandon the strategic path we are on as the conditions aren't conducive. I am guilty of that myself, sometimes focusing on monthly results and telling my team, "We've survived the month and can live on for another day!" I think it is rare to find ideal business timing when it comes to starting a journey to overcome difficult issues or drive a significant transformation. But if we don't start on that path now, when would be a good time?

There are times when decisive action is needed, but they must all work in line with the long game in mind. Some plans are so attractive that you would want to jump straight into implementing them, but this is a trap that a lot of Asian business leaders tend to fall into.

Step back and think about the persistent issues plaguing your business. Every industry and every company has a persistent issue, good or bad, surrounding them. What are those real-world issues and does the plan that you want to execute immediately address those issues? Or are you just focusing on sales and profit margins?

Clearly define the megatrends in your industry because these are the ones that the consumers are moving towards; they have momentum, and some are so ingrained that they will not go away. Instead of fighting these megatrends, how do you be a part of them? If you can formulate a plan that will (a) drive your own business, (b) integrate dealing with the issues surrounding your industry, and (c) participate in a megatrend whilst mitigating the risks, then you will probably have a more robust plan that is better actionable in this ever-evolving world.

I believe that if you use a lens of "Win the present, build the future" in your planning process, you will be able to frame up what parts of the business you need to focus on to get your short-term results and what initiatives you must start chipping away at to get to your longer-term transformation. If you have only one element without the other, the plan becomes a fragile and static one. It is also always helpful in the organisation to have a set of people focused on delivering the business today, and another set of people looking to future-proof the organisation.

Because change is always difficult, be sure that you are conscious about taking your people along this journey. Always have the pulse of the organisation to understand where things fit, where people stand, and how views are evolving. Check on the company culture and check on the alignment of values with vision. Then annually, review all your plans to ensure that everything is on target with your long-term plans. Even better, depending on your industry, review every quarter and check up on things as you go. At McDonald's, the five-year plan is reviewed every year to make sure that it is still sound. Perhaps in the first two years things are going swimmingly but by year three we are scrutinising it because there needs to be an adjustment of cost due to market forces.

In the end, the real measure is to ask ourselves if we have moved the needle toward our longer-term vision. Have we spent the last three years just comfortably administering the business, or have we been courageous and achieved good progress towards our transformation or vision?

A thought-starter I often use with my team: Three years from now, when we are sitting around our leadership table, will we, because of our inaction and kicking the can down the road, still be talking about the same set of issues and pontificating about how difficult it is to start on the changes required? Or would we have already started on this difficult journey and be saying to ourselves: "Thank goodness we made our moves. We are now in much better shape than we were before. We are in much better shape than our competitors." A leader with foresight and courage creates the momentum for change when it is appropriate and required.

ASIAN LEADERSHIP LEARNING
The Courage to Transform for Enduring Growth
Wern-Yuen Tan, CEO, PepsiCo APAC

Wern-Yuen Tan – or Yuen, as he is more commonly called – is one of the brightest Asian leaders that I have had the privilege to work with. I knew Yuen during his time at

McDonald's, working first as Head of Strategy for the APMEA (Asia Pacific, Middle East and Africa) region, and after that successfully helming the McDonald's Taiwan market as Managing Director. He has an impressive background to say the least, being an Oxford and Cambridge graduate, a Singapore Police Force Overseas Scholar, and having worked in the Singapore Police Force, the Singapore Ministry of Trade and Industry, and the Boston Consulting Group. His more recent operational and senior management roles include his time at McDonald's Taiwan, as President and CEO of Walmart China, and now as Chief Executive Officer of PepsiCo APAC. He concurrently sits on established boards and provides advisory to the industry at large.

Given his intellect and analytical background, Yuen's ability to apply critical thinking, and resolution, to complex issues is second to none. But what I admire most about him is his courageous shift towards operational roles, where he has had to not only craft out the vision and way forward for the enterprise, but to also do the heavy lifting of executing his plans and bringing his people and organisation along.

Yuen shared his career journey with me, and his notable personal development learnings include:

1. Being led by purpose. A leader must understand, and be true to, his real motivations for wanting to be in a specific organisation or taking on a specific role, and be clear how he can truly add value.

2. Taking control of your career and not being an "insecure over-achiever". Asians tend to believe that just because they do the hard and good work, they should be equally rewarded or promoted in a timely manner. This can sometimes be a false assumption in the competitive corporate world. Yuen always makes the effort to "show up" with intention, and to muster the confidence to showcase the good work that he and his teams achieve to earn their due recognition and place in the organisation.

3. Being courageous. Yuen is always challenging himself and his teams to seek new challenges, to operate and thrive outside of their comfort zones.

4. Being able to shift your leadership style – moving from detailed mastery (knowing every aspect of the business) to mastering the art of getting results through inspiring people and teams.

5. Creating an environment where team members can have uncomfortable conversations if needed, and turning these into opportunities to deliver value from diversity and inclusion.

One of Yuen's strengths has been his ability to shape the business and organisation such that the wheels turn to offer consistent annual performance achievement, while also generating multi-year momentum towards a transformational vision, which he and his team would have set for the business. A good example of this was manifested during his time in China.

When Yuen took on the role as President and CEO of Walmart, he entered the well-entrenched and successful Walmart system with new perspective and a keen sense of the marketplace behind his Asian upbringing and exposure. Being part of the largest global retailer, and with the massive opportunity in China, Yuen's first task was to continue Walmart's momentum and build upon the legacy and successful footprint that his predecessors had left behind.

To "win the present", Yuen's priority was to rally the organisation around the core of business, securing and opening the right-sized formats of Walmart stores across the vast geography and focusing on the product offerings that were most relevant to the Chinese consumer. This model was well aligned with the U.S. strategy and offered a long runway of growth, and it was mission-critical that the team focused on exceptional site development, everyday value pricing and differentiated customer offerings and services to gain even more market share.

Many a CEO would have been more than satisfied with the trajectory that this safe global strategy provided for the business. But China was at the time also rapidly changing, and faster than the rest of the world. Many retailers were entering the market at an accelerated pace, and the omnichannel and digital environment had become much more pervasive than any other market, especially with the rise of online behemoths like Alibaba and JD.com.

To "build the future", Yuen and his team determined that the business could not just sit comfortably, and that there was a need to begin the journey to differentiate their offerings from the growing competition while also transforming the traditionally offline and e-commerce business models into an integrated and seamless omnichannel approach. The idea then was to test and validate:

1. Expanding Sam's Club (Walmart's sister brand) more aggressively, via large-footprint membership club formats, complemented by "dark stores" to serve time-pressured consumers in urban centres. Sam's Clubs in China also adopted a locally differentiated strategy of serving the most affluent Chinese consumers, with a wide range of locally sourced private label products. This represented a significant departure from traditional membership club business models deployed internationally.

2. Setting an aggressive multi-year goal to become the first offline retailer to convert at least 70% of all transactions to digital transactions. This would enable deeper consumer insights, allowing Walmart to be

more agile in responding to consumer needs. Supported by data science, teams could then present the right product offerings to consumers via the most relevant touchpoints, ultimately improving customer satisfaction and loyalty.

Earlier in the book, we discussed how transformation and change require not only courage but also the ability of the leader to articulate the vision clearly and establish viability with facts to ensure that any new investment benefits from the right financial returns. Also, proof that the organisation can remain squarely focused and deliver on the core business, while at the same time being able to stretch and take on additional and new skillsets to get to the future opportunity. Suffice it to say that Yuen and his team had their fair share, and a mix of, debate, persuasion, pushback, scepticism, support, and encouragement within the system, both from global stakeholders as well as from local teams. The result after all the testing, work, validation, debate and eventual expansion of these initiatives was that the business in China now had more than just one traditional pillar of growth, and was in a much stronger position to compete in the marketplace, leveraging on:

1. The traditional core strength of the still-expanding Walmart business.

2. The new expansion of Sam's Club to differentiate the brand with more novel offerings versus the competition.

3. A significant omnichannel presence in step with evolving consumer purchasing behaviours; and now with a new digital organisation and infrastructure that could take advantage of the ever-changing digital trends and new opportunities, and real-time data that offered yet another new growth pillar for future consumer engagement and growth.

Finally, Yuen reminds us that many of these powerful local insights to the business are delivered by local leaders. The final make-or-break of these strategies is also executed by the local leaders. Global companies should thus be more deliberate in the lenses they take in assessing local talent and leadership – not just with the view of a leader that fits the Western mould, but a leader that can collaborate across geographies, and more importantly, have the right thought and people leadership that can be effective and relevant in the local marketplace. Clearly, we want local leadership that can perform on a larger stage, but at the same time we want top Asian leaders who are not just good at presenting in front of global stakeholders, but who can also draw the right local insights to allow businesses to be even more competitive and differentiated, and who can communicate (sometimes in the necessary local language), rally and inspire their local teams, stakeholders and partners towards excellent execution and a common cause.

When asked about what he thinks is his most differentiated advantage being an Asian leader in Asia, Yuen believes that it is his ability to sort through and develop the right talent that fits each nuanced Asian market, taking a thoughtful but pragmatic lens as to who would be best suited for the role and the contextual setting. As we win the present and build the future for our businesses, we must pay as much heed to building the future of the right Asian talent as they will be the ones carrying us through to the finish line and ensuring the long-term sustainability of the brand.

Key Takeaways for Asian Leaders

- Be a strong advocate for the fundamental global brand strategy and business model. You were placed in that position by the enterprise to be its steward, advocate and guardian. Never forget that.

- Maximise your local sense of the marketplace coupled with fact-based assessment to understand and identify key insights and changing megatrends that may not be as visible to stakeholders sitting outside of the market. You're sited nearer to the field after all, and that's the incremental value you must offer.

- Offer an articulate vision for change and/or transformation that would augur well for the future of the business, and be courageous in championing your ideas, while also having the discipline to test, validate and bring your stakeholders along what might sometimes be an uncomfortable journey, and one that would call for change and involve some level of risk.

- Don't launch and leave. Stick with your convictions (if they are educated ones) as change sometimes comes with start-stops, doubters and scepticism along the way. However, fall in the love with the problem (keep plugging away at trying to solve it) rather than your solution.

Key Takeaways for Global Organisations

- Have a fair expectation that your person on the ground will protect the brand and be a guardian of the global business model.

- Adopt an open mindset that the same objectives and success in foreign markets might be achieved by different approaches which resonate better with local consumers. Different markets might start with different assumptions – for example affordability, product knowledge, education, cultural variations, regulations.

- Encourage a "reverse-boomerang" of ideas and innovation – not all best practices have to flow from West to East. Make an account of how many great practices from Asia are shared within the larger system, especially in relation to data management and technology, with digital adoption and practices being more wholeheartedly embraced by consumers in Asia.

- Don't use a one-size-fits-all assessment of talent based on just global standards for senior talent. Make thoughtful allowances for local context, language, and cultural values to complement the proven talent models.

CHAPTER 7

Gatekeeping Excellence

"The lonely road to greatness is better than
the crowded road to mediocrity."
MATSHONA DHLIWAYO

ONE ASPECT OF the typical Asian mindset that can be very detrimental to organisations is the tendency to avoid confrontation. We are just not good at it! When we see something that is not up to our standards, we tend to take a long time to correct it because we beat around the bush before getting to the point. Too many Asians do not like to rock the boat. But if you have a leader who sets the tone for keeping standards high, you can change this culture. Once a leader accepts mediocrity or lowers the standards, everyone else will follow. But if everybody understands that there *is* somebody who is going to maintain a high level of excellence, then most will strive to give of their best at every point in time.

If you expect high-quality work from your people, my experience has been that the strong performers will almost always return that expectation with an outcome that surpasses even your expectation. Over time, these stronger performers will also come to realise that they are capable of so much more and continue to ride their cycle of success by setting their own high standards. Hopefully, this leads to fulfilment, empowerment, and a strong sense of achievement. The folks that respond well are keepers! They are the ones who, when given a task, come back with thoughtful, creative and quality ideas and execution. They check their own standards.

And holding standards high is not just in the realm of doing things. You should expect quality analysis, quality thinking, quality planning. You do not want mediocre ideas or bog-standard observations to filter through in discussions. Are we just implementing things that everybody else is implementing? Why can't we spend that extra time to research and get better insights? Foster a culture of thinking a bit harder and more critically, get that much more creative, to find the ideas or solutions that are robust and thus able to sustain themselves for the longer term.

Holding Standards High

In the hospitality industry, anything and everything can go wrong. The death spiral happens when we think we must be nice to people and only recognise and congratulate people while never pointing out challenges and issues. In a system like at McDonald's, where we have standards already set up in terms of expectations of what we need to serve to the customer, the leader sets the tone of what those standards are.

If I walk into a restaurant and I see something wrong, but I do not say anything about it, I would have let that standard drop and allowed the issue to fester. So it is imperative that I communicate to the staff the problem I have spotted. Now, how we communicate must necessarily be mindful of the issues that the staff themselves face. The goal here is to communicate effectively that we are aware of the issues that lead to a slipping of standards, and we will work to mitigate them and help them resolve it, while affirming that this slipping up is not acceptable.

Why are the French Fries not crispy? Why is there litter on the floor of the restaurants? Why are the lines too long? There are multiple reasons why these things happen, and there needs to be empathy and understanding when correcting these problems. We must adopt a Heads Up view to our frontliners. Turnover is very high in this type of industry, and while we as an organisation are veterans, the same is not true of the on-the-ground staff. It is typical that each year sees more than 50% turnover, with new faces joining us every day. The cadence of systemised training, of repetition and drills, must be maintained to ensure that every staff knows what is expected.

Speak Up

The Asian tendency to fear contradicting The Boss is not going to be conducive for bold and success-making ideas. To foster a culture of moving towards excellence, we need to encourage people to speak up and be unafraid to do so. There should be an understanding that there will be no consequences for speaking up, even if it means contradicting what the boss said. Of course, this is all with the understanding that it needs to be constructive and add value to the discussion. With that said, opinions should also be encouraged because we need to listen to the different voices in the organisation. We may not agree with everything, but at least be respectful of every opinion.

We need to create a culture in Asia that drives the idea that we should never be static. And to move forward, every opinion counts. If it is a flat idea, call it out! That is what is needed. We need people who can point out that the emperor has no clothes, that it is just a mediocre idea and that we can do better.

Town halls in Western countries are very different. Apart from having a good agenda set right from the start, everybody jumps in to either acknowledge the idea being tabled or to find ways to enhance and build on it. In Western countries, there is the notion of building upon an idea and making it better. But over in Asia, everybody simply accepts an idea for what it is, no matter if they believe in it or not. If they don't, there is always the corridor talk where people let out their true feelings, but that is not conducive to progress. Or worse, blind execution happens straight after.

Here is an example that illustrates this mentality well. We were in the process of planning to run a BTS K-pop promotion during the Covid-19 period, right at the peak of the infectious Delta cases. The Singapore government at that point in time was limiting interactions and gatherings to curb the rising daily cases. It just so happened that the launch date for the promotion happened to be right smack in the middle of this crisis and could not be pushed out any further due to contractual requirements. We had a meeting to discuss how we were going to execute the launch, especially in managing the crowds in the restaurants. We had seen what happened in neighbouring countries, with hordes of people descending on the restaurants, and we were worried about how we were going to handle the lines and crowds.

In my mind, I thought we were going to do it via delivery and drive-thru, as it was not the right time for crowds to be forming in our restaurants for dine-in or takeaway. But things did not turn out that way at the discussion. People were just talking about how we were going to manage the long lines and doing the launch in-person, in-store. I was just waiting for someone to say something to the contrary. It was not the right action to take, and we were going to get killed by the media and by the authorities and by all the negative press for causing crowds at every McDonald's restaurant. But because one of the project leaders said, "Let's discuss how we are going to get the full suite of execution done at the restaurants", everybody simply followed suit.

After the circular discussion had gone on for 45 minutes, I could not sit with my mouth shut any longer. I asked if anyone thought what we were doing was a bad idea. And then I sat back and watched what happened next. Folks finally began speaking up, claiming that they, too, were not confident that they could control the ungated crowds, and that we might get in trouble with the authorities if these crowds then led to a super-spreader event.

Why didn't anyone speak up earlier? It is because they thought that was what the boss wanted, so they would try fervently to execute it.

But it is not about doing things right, it is about doing the right things. And we need to have the temerity to speak up when we know it is going to go very badly for the organisation. We need to get rid of that mentality where if the boss wants it, we must figure out a way to get exactly what she wants. This herd mentality is dangerous in the long term, and one cannot have just one voice in an organisation. Just think of all the unspeakable atrocities that have happened in world history because people were "just following orders".

We should always be able to call on people to share different points of view. Diversity generates creativity. One of the tricks I use before we go into a contentious debate is to socialise ideas with various groups of my leadership team, and with a few people that have different points of view. I solicit their individual viewpoints before the meeting and encourage them to share these at the meeting.

People need to share their point of view, and while I might have a solution in my mind, I want everybody to say something because we can all benefit from the sharing of different perspectives. There could be better ideas, or even the germination of ideas when different ones come into contact, and minds could be changed.

Dare to Be Different

In this second part of the book, I laid out fundamental areas where I believe Asian leaders need to reflect more on as they embark on senior leadership roles, especially within global organisations. In the next section of the book, I will discuss how we exert these fundamentals and bring our people and organisations along with us in times of stability, or in times of crisis and transformation.

As Asians in charge, we have a lot to learn from the leadership and management examples already out there and in practice. But as we do, we also need to find our own authentic voice. There are already too many who work through the common checklist on what they think is correct for leaders to do versus walking down the lonelier path of ignoring the noise and doing the right things.

A clear example is what can be observed with corporate communication these days. With the need to be politically correct (and I can understand some public circumstances where this would be required), we have been deluged with the same corporate speak and jargon across leaders and organisations that at the end of the day becomes white noise and does little to inspire. There are fewer conversations that come from a place of authenticity, fewer words that are spoken from the heart. But in fact, this is needed more than ever today as we face an increasingly uncertain and volatile world.

You can make the choice not to flow along these safe currents, and instead offer a leadership style that is unique to you, that is different from the cookie-cutter leader. You have a choice and must be courageous to offer a leadership brand that is effective and empathetic while setting yourself apart from the rest. Why be normal? Dare to be different!

PART 3

Asian Leadership in a VUCA World

CHAPTER 8

It's About People

"Leadership is about making others better
as a result of your presence and making sure
that impact lasts in your absence."
SHERYL SANDBERG

IN THIS ERA of so much volatility, transformation and disruption, the leader's role in shaping a living and breathing organisation to be battle-ready is paramount. The enterprise at its core must synthesise the company's vision and translate that into strong execution, while at its flanks there must be the resiliency to flex, adapt and stay nimble amidst changing circumstances.

Shaping the Organisation

Picture this: You have just been hired to take on a new high-flying leadership role and you are now figuring out your game plan. What is the first thing on your mind? It is more than likely that you will focus on the hard aspects of how to grow the business, what strategies you will employ, how aggressive you should drive targets, and how you might compete more effectively.

I believe that would lead to an outstanding start, getting the business end of things sorted out so that your team has clarity and can get going on the set-out direction. Most Asians, and most executives, naturally focus and spend their time and energy on achieving this growth and financial KPIs. The hard numbers lead to annual plan achievements and corresponding job security, remuneration and/or better career prospects.

But what comes next? How do we enable the achievement of these important business goals? It should be evident what the answer is: through our people. Often, we take for granted that the organisation in its current state will be able to deliver results. Thinking about shaping the organisation to win the present but also build the future constantly takes a backseat. And then when things do not go the way they should, we wonder why our people cannot get the job done despite being handed what we think is good business direction.

As Asian leaders stepping into senior roles, we must be mindful that building organisation capability and culture stands on equal footing as having a great business plan. If you have a plan that does not have a robust focus on people and organisation, then I suggest that your plan is on shaky ground, like a house of cards. Having a plan to shape the organisation is also not something for a later time. It is something to jump straight into at the get-go because it is critical for great execution. Identifying great talent, building trust, relationships, teamwork, and instilling values and culture just takes that much longer, often lagging business pace. So, no time like the present to start!

Most leaders may not be immediately aware that the higher you go up the ladder, the more of your time should be spent in this area. While coaching many senior executives and direct reports, I consistently get told that the most diffi-cult part of their jobs is not necessarily framing up the busi-ness, but more of managing their people, getting their teams to gel, urging the employees to take more initiative, getting them to perform at a higher level, keeping them motivated, and so on. The question I pose to them (assuming the busi-ness strategy is firmly in place) is this: "You say that manag-ing people and teams causes you the biggest headache, yet also represents the biggest opportunity for more optimal per-formance – but how much of your time is *actually* spent on cultivating this environment where your people can thrive?"

This understanding will be new to a lot of young lead-ers. It certainly did not come instantly to me as I advanced through the ranks. I was very much focused on the num-bers, performing at a higher level and wanting to make a mark with a show of strong results. As I took on higher roles of senior leadership and P&L responsibilities, I was always reminded by leaders on the business end that I had to make tough decisions, sometimes people ones, for the enterprise to succeed. Making tough decisions was viewed as a rite of passage and represented a coming of age. No one drilled me with similar passion that I needed to also shape and nurture my organisation. I guess that would have sounded a bit soft.

I believe I have a good feel for people. I held leader-ship roles in school, in university, and in the army, and I was comfortable with working with diverse groups. When I took on my first real top leadership role as Managing Director of

McDonald's Singapore in 2004, I was fortunate to be handed an organisation that was filled with talented and tenured employees, that had a culture of excellence built over 25 years. Sure, I could help make some improvements here and there, but it was overall in good shape.

My real "A-ha! moment" on the need to think more carefully about organisation development was when I went to China. We already had a base of 1,000 restaurants there and a sizeable organisation of 50,000 people. As described earlier, we had an aggressive multi-year growth plan of adding a few thousand more restaurants, which would translate to adding on a few hundred thousand employees. We were on the ground floor of growth and organisation building, and we needed to be sure we laid a solid infrastructure for the former, and good systems and culture for the latter. From an organisation standpoint, how could we best structure our teams to meet our business direction? How could we encourage self-sufficient teams that moved along the business path with minimal supervision? How could we encourage discussion and innovation while also staying focused on execution? What was the right culture that we should set for our future organisation?

There are too many aspects of shaping an organisation to possibly cover. Below, I will touch on the few key areas where I think Asian leaders would benefit the most from applying their energy.

The "Smell" of the Workplace

The culture and energy of the workplace is set by your leadership tone – the behaviours that you encourage, and those that you will not tolerate. Are you aware of, and are you deliberate in, the tone that you are setting at the top? To create a living, sustainable organisation that will operate for many years, you must create the right environment for it to thrive. A leader cannot expect his team to consistently produce great results if they have to work in conditions that are not conducive for them. Without the right culture in place, you will not get the performance you desire.

The late Professor Sumantra Ghoshal offered a very apt metaphor for management styles during a World Economic Forum talk at Davos in 1995.[10] He talked of the times when he would visit Calcutta during the summer months. Calcutta is a wonderful place, but the downtown environment there in summer – high temperatures, humidity, and dust – always drained him, made him feel tired and lethargic. Contrast that with the times he would visit France, and the Fontainebleau Forest in the spring. The environment there with its beautiful scenery and fresh air always made him feel alive and put a spring in his step.

This is the same person placed in two very different environments, in two different contexts. The "smell" and sense of each place evokes different feelings and emotions. While we might have good talent with us, how are we as leaders creating a "smell" for the workplace that energises and revitalises them to be the best that they can be, and not demoralise them towards apathy.

An environment that is based on Constraint, Compliance, Control and Contract – Prof Ghoshal likened this to a stifling, draining summer in Calcutta. One that instead fosters an environment of Stretch, Self-discipline, Support and Trust is akin to an invigorating jaunt through the Fontainebleau Forest in spring.

Stifling Summer in Calcutta Context

Constraint:
: Where the staff is restricted by a set of rigid constraints.

Compliance:
: Where there are rigid and befuddling systems in place forcing compliance from the staff. Think of the "follow SOP[11] only" mindset that leaves little room for flexibility.

Control:
: Where the management seeks to only control the employee.

Contract:
: Where every form of relationship existing within the organisation is contractual in nature and emphasised as such: the contract between employer and employee, the contract that needs to be negotiated for a salary raise, the budget contract, and so on.

Invigorating Spring in Fontainebleau Forest Context

Stretch: Where every individual in the company tries to do more, thanks to an excellent and exciting set of values created by the management.

Self-discipline: Where every individual displays self-discipline without the need for enforced constraints; rather, it springs from a company culture of embedded norms of self-discipline.

Support: Where the senior management does not seek to control; rather, they support and guide everyone in the organisation.

Trust: Where trust is the basis of every relationship within the organisation, instead of being merely contractual.

How much deliberate effort we put into creating the right "smell" for our enterprise is as important as developing our business and financial goals.

Building Self-Sufficient Teams

Think of the North Star that Belinda Wong discussed earlier in the book. Each little vessel or ship is moving towards that same direction; they may not be following the exact same path, but each knows where they are headed and how to get there. People and teams have their own identities, voices and characters. Once they are aligned on the key direction, we should strive to allow them to exert their best abilities, creativity and persistence to achieve success towards the collective goal. Some will fare better than others, and those that do will be recognised and rewarded accordingly. We should avoid the temptation to throw down the iron fist of control just because we are wary of the few non-performers who might wander astray (of course they should be monitored and managed separately).

I referenced the right-side-up organisation earlier on, in Chapter 1, where our role as leaders should be about setting direction, providing resources, and creating the right environment for the organisation to succeed. Our business units closer to the frontline should be self-starters in providing customer satisfaction and executing for results. As I try and empower my people down the line, I strive for three disciplines to be in place:

1. Be organised.

2. Have constant and consistent one-on-one alignment and communication.

3. Share leadership.

In being organised, I try to first be sure that the business plan is as strong as it can be, and not have to change because we didn't give it our best effort during the planning stage. I see a lot of organisations who change their plans on a dime and attribute the need for change to different circumstances or in the name of being nimble. Constant plan changes lead to last-minute execution, causing frustration down the line. If the context indeed has changed, then by all means change the plan too. But if it is because of lazy or bad planning (not anticipating the situation, not laying down a plan that was strong enough), then shame on the leaders who didn't get the job done. Thanks to them, everyone in the organisation must now move left or right at the drop of a hat.

Being planful can also be a strong competitive advantage. I often debate with some of our startup partners who profess their nimbleness to the extent that they don't have a plan for even the following month as they want to remain fluid. If that is what it takes for a startup to succeed (which I do not necessarily believe), then so be it. But I often also always remind them that we take the starting approach of a strong, well-thought-out plan, and then commit to executing the heck out of it because we now have lead-time to execute the elements – and with lead-time we execute very well.

With a plan, we are also able to generate and hold on to momentum. By the time our competitors react to our current strong initiative, we are already on to the next one that we have planned for and already in execution mode, thereby gaining even more traction and momentum. We always want to be ahead in execution, and not be caught on the back foot.

Finally, in being organised, I am always aware of and respectful of people's time. I review my calendar constantly to be sure that I provide enough time for my people to get back to me on requests (minimises last-minute whim-and-fancy requests), and am always early or at least on time for meetings. As leaders, we need to be sure we prioritise the work of our people ahead of our own. I'm known by my team members as Mr No Rush because I start all my requests of them with "No rush...". By being organised ourselves, it gives our teams and people a chance to organise their own work and be self-sufficient without being bogged down by fire-fighting changes and last-minute requests. We need to be respectful of our people's time.

To allow for self-sufficiency, it is imperative that there is continuous alignment along the way. I find monthly scheduled one-on-one sessions with my direct reports extremely helpful for achieving this. In the focused and private time that we have together, we align our goals, discuss issues, coach each other on areas of opportunity, bounce off ideas and leave the meeting with a clear sense of what to do next, that's fully aligned. There should be little surprise about what follows, and thus little disruption to what will be executed. And because we are in full alignment, my direct reports can take the lead and responsibility on the tasks at hand.

Which leads to my last discipline: sharing leadership. I never want to usurp my subordinate's authority to lead their parts of the business. Our one-on-one alignment process certainly helps with that, and we actively draw up clear RACI (Responsible, Accountable, Consulted, Informed) charts to give the organisation clarity on who leads what, and who makes the final decisions on which projects. When a project is progressing well, I am first to recognise the leader of the project, and when it's not going so well, we talk about it in our one-on-one sessions.

As the senior leader in the organisation, I am always asked to receive awards on behalf of the company or hand out awards to recognise our teams. I make it a point to let my different direct reports actively engage in these ceremonies, because they lead their teams and should be more visible as the ones being recognised or offering the recognition. By sharing leadership, you get more buy-in from your leadership teams and that in turn encourages shared accountability and success.

Offer Recognition and Empathy in Abundance

A vibrant organisation thrives on positivity, even in the face of adversity. As part of McDonald's 40th anniversary in Singapore, one of the four legacy gifts we committed to was the Gift of Recognition. We know that in the service industry, anything on any given day can go wrong. We spend a lot of time understanding the underlying issues and coaching to resolve problems. We never put our heads in the sand to ignore or walk by an issue.

So instead of a culture of catching people doing things wrong, we decided to create a culture of catching them doing things right! And then we recognised them for it, and shared their stories. We started a RICO (Recognising Individuals Constantly and Openly) movement to recognise our people at every opportunity. When we visit restaurants, we bring along fun and exclusive collar pins to give to the folks as we recognise them in front of their peers. We publish monthly great deeds done by our Hospitality Heroes with the hope also that these good deeds spur on the rest of the organisation to emulate them. And we have annual awards that showcase the best of the best.

Having empathy for your people in the face of business pressure is also one of the most important traits that a leader needs to develop. I will discuss more on empathy when we cover the learnings from the Covid-19 crisis in Chapter 10. Being able to have a sense of how your employees are feeling, how the organisation is faring, putting yourself in their shoes – having a strong sense and pulse of your organisation allows you to make better decisions. Having empathy for all levels ("I see you") engenders trust and loyalty.

Every time we make an announced visit to a restaurant, I know that the team would have likely spent hours or even days preparing. So I always make it a point when I first enter the restaurant to go around all areas to personally greet every one of our crew and managers – one, because it's just good manners, and two, because I know they want to show off the best of themselves when the "boss" is in the house. So, let's give them the opportunity to do so. Only after that would we get into discussions with the restaurant manager on business matters.

In 2018, we encountered an incident that was widely circulated on social media of a customer abusing one of our young employees. I believe we might have frustrated the customer, but the manager very quickly came out to resolve the issue and fix the problem. Despite this, the customer continued to berate our young employee, used vulgar language to scold him, and at times posed a physical threat. Throughout this episode, I was proud that the team of managers protected the young employee, kept their cool, tried to appease the customer and never once crossed the line of being rude.

This incident also surfaced the frustrations of our internal people and those in the service industry. Is the customer always right? Do we have to take their abuse? I thought it was important to address this sentiment immediately. I made it a point to inform our system folks that as a company we would always be customer-oriented, but we would at the same time not tolerate any mistreatment of our people. I told them to never cross the line in any of our approaches, but if they felt they could not serve a belligerent customer, then so be it, and make the call. This small show of support really resonated with our people. They were heartened that the leaders understood and more importantly acknowledged the loss of respect that frontliners sometimes must contend with and appreciated the fact that we would have their backs!

Providing Empathy, Building Trust and Being Respectful are three of the important attributes we must genuinely offer as leaders, especially as our workplaces and social environments become increasingly diverse, and sometimes more divergent. Remember that the decisions we make are not only business ones – we are also making human decisions. In the many years of interacting with my colleagues, and in all situations of celebratory or challenging circumstances, I have always tried to live up to what the American poet Maya Angelou so elegantly stated: "People will forget what you said, people will forget what you did, but people will never forget how you made them feel."

CHAPTER 9

Be an Inspired Communicator

"Communicate your passion clearly,
concisely, and with genuine conviction."
RICHARD BRANSON

A S THE WORLD, and our workplaces, face dramatic changes with shortened business cycles, technological disruptions, and ever-increasing levels of global and environmental volatility, it is important that we pair our efforts in strengthening our organisations (as described in the chapter before) with a stronger cadence of communication throughout the organisation. This will ensure that a free flow of communication activities can take place in times of stability or in times of crisis. As Asian leaders, we must also personally work towards developing a more inspiring communication style that can offer clarity and impact amidst a variety of these exigencies.

One of the common watchouts Asians leaders must avoid is the tendency to just communicate linear instructions and generic information – the "I say, you do" approach. Sure, it is efficient, takes less time, and doesn't require you to provide any rationale or gain buy-in. But the path that we should aspire to is one where we communicate with impact to motivate, inspire and bring people and the organisation along with passion. We should strive for this at every given opportunity when meeting with our stakeholders.

Communication from Leadership

I'm certainly not the best orator, and as I mentioned earlier, not the best at speaking off the cuff. Whenever I provide some leadership perspective or give a speech to my teams, I continue to have the bad habit of only finalising the speech at the last moment, even though I might have started prepa-rations much earlier. The area that often gets me stuck is not the information or content – I am clear and confident about what needs to be disseminated.

What I am often not satisfied with is how to share that information with clarity and simplicity, while at the same time offering powerful and relevant messaging that would make the audience sit up and listen. Will the audience be excited, energised and inspired by what I am saying? I find that simply delivering a message is easy, but delivering one that is targeted at the right level for audience understand-ing and motivation is much more difficult and requires more deliberate effort.

When an audience listens to a relatively generic and uninspired speech, the message flows through like a narrow funnel. Only a portion of the audience would have listened to what was said, an even smaller portion would have under-stood what was said, and the smallest portion would put what was said into any kind of action.

The key to effective communication, then, is not just about disseminating the idea; it's about elevating the messag-ing and delivery in terms that the audience can relate to, be inspired by, and want to act on. Because many Asians don't tend to show up with big personalities or strong showmanship skills, it might take more time to craft our messaging.

For my part, I socialise some of the topics I might share with various constituents and see what resonates and what just doesn't stick, and adjust my approach accordingly. I supplement my sometimes dry delivery with the use of visuals and pictures which might be funny, illustrate the point better, or evoke a stronger response; or the use of videos to break the monotony of the speech while more effectively bringing the ideas to life. I have found also that showcasing photos of the people whom you are addressing in the conversation, or telling them stories about themselves, draws them in. Whatever it takes, put in the effort to relate better, to energise and to rally your people to action.

You do of course have to back up what you say with follow-through action – it cannot just be about inspirational words with no outcome. In communication, it is not only about what is being said, but who the messenger is. So be sure you have already worked on your credibility, of always delivering on what you say you would do.

Every communication opportunity is an opportunity to inspire, to showcase your leadership, to lead. To that end, the high communication standard I set for myself as I try to knock every communication session out of the park is this: Every time I am on the speaking agenda, I want the audience to be filled with excitement and anticipation because (from past experience) they are expecting that I will be doing my best to make it captivating, relevant, informative and touch an emotion in them.

Communication with Stakeholders

The other side of effective leadership communication is the ability to articulate with clarity *upwards* to your stakeholders – your bosses, shareholders, investors. Many a time, these stakeholders are situated in other geographies, and would certainly not be as close to the heart of the business or issues as you are. Be aware of that in your communication.

In my experience, Asian executives tend to quickly jump into the fray of the discussion before first taking a breath and providing perspective or placing the discussion in context – it's a discussion without head or tail. We must remember that our bosses, busy CEOs, or board investors, have many other responsibilities and businesses that they deal with daily. Yours is just one of many. Your market is one of many markets they have responsibility for. While critically important to you, your issue might not even be on their radar. So make it easier for them by providing the objective of the discussion, some background, perspective and local context, so that they can begin the conversation at the same starting point as you.

It is also good practice to informally socialise topics that you anticipate are complex or might lead to difficult decisions that need to be made. Best to have these informal and timely check-ins before the formal process of presentation and decision-making takes place. This practice has helped me navigate through many tough decisions with stakeholders that had to be made – for example on people or on business direction at the board or management level.

Another trait that Asians tend to have is not being precise and clear about what we are trying to convey. We don't summarise our thoughts with a clear headline but instead let the conversation meander with convoluted explanations before – hopefully – landing on the point we want to make. This is in contrast to the linear communication style practised in the West:

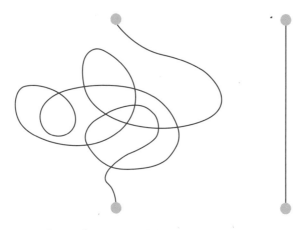

Differences between East (left) and West (right) in communicating opinions, adapted from a visualisation by Professor Yang Liu[12]

There is a great discipline in communication – and in particular, writing – that Procter & Gamble used to require of its brand managers. One, every memo should be no longer than a page. You must be able to express your thoughts, findings or requests on a single page. This practice promotes efficiency in thought and communication. Two, every paragraph should start with an underlined headline that summarises what you want to say in the ensuing text. This forces you to really think about the essence of the message.

I often face these communication issues with some of the people I coach, even senior leaders. So, for those who have a little more difficulty with clarity, I employ a bit of formality in our sessions (which they don't like!), so that they can put into practice a structured approach to our conversations. For each communication session, I ask them to:

1. Set an agenda prior to the meeting (to prevent topic meandering).

2. State the objective and outcome.

3. Start with perspective and context before we jump into the topic.

4. Lead with the headline of each topic before getting into the meat of it.

5. Process the meeting at the end of it to see what went well, and what can be improved on.

6. Practise using mind-maps to help structure more complex discussions and to better explain issues.

It is quite amazing to see the improvement by just having a bit of thought discipline. Your stakeholders will appreciate the clarity, understanding and efficiency of the communication session. It will lead them to be better able to understand your issues, support you, and provide you with the resources you need.

Finally, in interacting with stakeholders, make sure to listen to their questions with intent, and answer thoughtfully. Direct and straightforward questions have easy answers. But I have seen many times that when someone senior asks a broader question, the Asian executive nervously bolts to an immediate and unconsidered answer. The retort he usually gets back is: "You're not listening to the question." This watchout may stem from our being brought up to answer questions directly and literally, as if sitting for an exam. In our minds, there must be an answer, and importantly, a correct one. We give less consideration to what might be behind the question or what perspective the stakeholder has in asking that question. Sometimes our answer may not be definitive; it may be an educated opinion or a judgment call – and that might just be what your stakeholders are seeking.

Just as it is important to make an impact at every employee session, it is even more imperative to make every stakeholder interaction a positive one. Prepare well. You see them less often, and every meeting is a valuable opportunity to establish trust and confidence in your leadership. How and what you communicate is the bridge to that understanding.

CHAPTER 10

Crisis Reveals True Leadership

"Don't let a good crisis go to waste."
WINSTON CHURCHILL

LIKE MANY OF THE concepts used today in business, "VUCA" came to us from the military. In 1987, based off the leadership theories of Warren Bennis and Burt Nanus, the U.S. Army War College coined the acronym at the end of the Cold War to describe the condition of the world at that time.[13]

VUCA stands for Volatility, Uncertainty, Complexity and Ambiguity. Those of you reading this who lived through those years should remember well the political climate of the era, particularly since the proxy wars of the Cold War were taking place in our neighbouring countries. The VUCA world is even more relevant today as we grapple with the effects of the Covid-19 pandemic, as global superpowers jockey for position, as technology disrupts traditional sectors, as inequality widens, and as the world heads towards a climate crisis.

Every year when we try to make plans, we are never certain that yet another monkey wrench, such as Covid-19, won't just come flying in to disrupt everything. Is there a black swan just around the corner that is just as likely to disrupt you as proffer new opportunities? It is ultimately a world that we must learn to navigate through and learn quickly how to mitigate any problems that will surely come our way.

My Experience with Crises

You can imagine that in my 25 years of working in the restaurant industry – where we deal daily with handling food, serving millions of customers, managing thousands of employees, working with hundreds of partners up and down the supply and logistics chain, regulators, and market authorities – I would have faced my fair share of crises big and small. I certainly have. Two major ones come to mind, which I will describe broadly but won't go into too much detail as there remains sensitive subject matter. But I will try and share my learnings from these incidents and show that all the leadership skills I have talked about for Asian leaders were essential in successfully steering my organisation through them.

First, a supply chain crisis in China. A big media exposé exploded on screens across the country about a supplier to a few major brands, including ours, that had been conducting errant practices in their production facility. These practices were conducted off-book and went under the radar despite all our stringent checks and audits on them. Soon telephones were ringing off the hook with regulators angrily demanding an explanation as to what was going on; there was strong consumer backlash on social media; employees and franchisees were up in arms; and our global HQ a continent away was demanding constant and real-time updates. There was intense pressure from every direction, and I knew that if we did not act fast, this crisis would bury the brand.

It was a call that not everyone was onboard with, but as the market CEO I made the judgement to stop supply from this supplier entirely. This was a significant partner to us and with that decision, we lost 60% of our protein supply in one fell swoop. I felt we had to bite this bullet, even though it would be a huge blow for us in the short term. We had to stand by our principles of placing food and customer safety first and now was the time to muster the courage to respond with values-first action. This was one of the most painful decisions we had to make, but I knew ultimately that this painful choice was necessary for us to have any chance of recovering the brand. And boy what a blow that was! Business dropped by 40% almost immediately. Catastrophe after catastrophe followed as the interconnectedness of the business ensured that almost everything fell when one key factor, the supply chain, was taken out.

But it was game face on, and we made sure that everyone remained level-headed as we moved into crisis management. By taking a customer-first approach, and by having a recovery plan to "Win the present and build the future", we recovered at a much faster rate than our competitors who were similarly affected. The entire crisis lasted about six months and gave us a crash course on the importance of rising above the fray. But it made the brand and organisation even stronger as a result.

The second significant crisis was one which all of us faced more recently, Covid-19. I recounted earlier in the book the harrowing circumstances of closing all our restaurants for three weeks, the first time in McDonald's 40-year history in Singapore that this had ever happened. With my experience of the earlier supply chain crisis, as well as having been through the SARS crisis in 2003, I was able to call on relevant learnings and strategies to develop a Crisis Management and Business Continuity plan. Because the past strategies were well captured, we were able to adapt and apply them in quick time, and share this blueprint globally for other markets to learn.

As I write this book, the pandemic appears to soon be moving into an endemic phase. The business has survived, thrived, and the transformations we have undertaken have made the organisation and brand stronger and more resilient than before.

Leading in a Crisis

There are many facets to dealing with a crisis, and there are many more expert views on how to navigate through them. I want to list down some practical learnings from my set of experiences. And again, I believe leading in a crisis effectively offers a great showcase that draws on all the leadership skills I have talked about which Asian leaders can embrace more of.

Leading in a Crisis vs Just Managing a Crisis

Managing a crisis is reactionary and every move is a response to a situation, but that means we are always on the back foot. Leading in a crisis addresses the issues at hand, but also anticipates next moves, next steps and provides a pathway to the best outcome for the organisation. It is about staying one step ahead.

Quickly Organise Teams for Business-Not-As-Usual

Crisis situations almost always evolve in unforeseen directions, leading to unexpected or dramatic consequences. It is mission-critical to be able to deal with the crisis at hand while also making sure that the business continues on course.

When Covid-19 came to Singapore's shores, we scenario-planned that it might take some time to resolve. So we organised ourselves very quickly into teams that would lead the crisis, and teams that would make sure that the operating business lights stayed on. We put in place a Covid-19 task force that would be the gatekeeper of all Covid-19-related updates and protocols and set the direction for all health and safety policies in step with the authorities' recommendations and mandates. We knew there would be lots of scenario-planning required along the way, and we set a team up to review and revise our plans and financials as the pandemic impacted our business on multiple fronts. We knew that there would be many people policies and compensation matters that we would need to address and deploy – government support, stop-work actions, managing the inflow and out-flow of labour, etc. – and we set up a team to oversee that for the organisation. These were just some examples of teams that were kept in place throughout the pandemic while the rest of us remained focused on the core business of looking after our customers and running the restaurants.

Establish Principles to Guide Action During a Crisis

In times of uncertainty, alignment across the organisation is key. Everyone needs to know how to behave, or what decisions to make in an immediate situation. Principles guide us as we balance our commercial needs with the needs of our stakeholders and our values.

In the early days of the Covid-19 crisis, for example, we drew up clear guiding principles so that everyone could be aligned as to what we hold most important and how we would act, such as:

- Ensure that customer and employee safety remain top priority above all else.

- Be a strong, authentic, and visible community partner in the crisis.

- Keep the system – shareholders, employees, business partners – consistently informed and energised for the long fight ahead.

- Leave no restaurant behind.

- Ensure business continuity with sustainable levels of cashflow, and a continued drive to close the gap on business performance.

- Gain market share in a challenged retail environment by being relevant and, most importantly, empathetic to the situation.

Be Visible

In a crisis, it is important for leaders to be visible and to be upfront in communicating to the organisation: what's going on, how we see events unfolding, what our concerns are. And to answer the all-important question for the organisation: Is there light at the end of the tunnel? Honesty is critical in this circumstance. Share openly the challenges faced. Rally the organisation to focus on the most important priorities. And most importantly, provide confidence and clarity on how we can move forward, together.

Teamwork and Diversity in a Crisis

There is no substitute for facing a crisis with a team that works well together, that supports each other, and that goes the extra mile for one another. As we talked about creating the positive and energised "smell" of the organisation, teamwork is something we need to work towards and foster during good times, and not to rue the lack of it when it is desperately needed during a crisis. Everyone needs to pull their weight in a crisis, to remove any department barriers and to have each other's backs.

Also critical is not having only people on the team who agree or only say "yes" in a crisis, or who cannot provide different perspectives, field perspectives or customer perspectives. An organisation adopting a one-track mind can only lead to wrong decisions and critical mistakes being made — ivory-tower decisions that have less empathy. Diverse views must be encouraged, and again this culture should be fostered in good times, before a crisis happens.

Lead with Empathy

While a crisis throws up challenging business concerns, it is important that we also put a human face to it. In managing the Covid-19 crisis for McDonald's in Singapore, we made sure to put ourselves in the shoes of our people:

- How did our foreign employees feel, given that they hadn't seen their families and loved ones for years?

- How about our senior employees, who were more vulnerable to the virus; our younger employees, who had not faced crises before and might be mentally stressed; or our working-parent employees, whose kids were attending school lessons from home?

- How did our restaurant teams in locations most affected, like downtown CBD or tourist areas, feel about their more dramatic drop in business – especially while their peers in the heartlands were performing better?

While we may not be able to address every constituent's concern to their fullest extent, we remain empathetic, balancing business policies with human polices that can be for the greater good.

Finally, in facing any crisis as a leader, be aware that the level of "noise" from the organisation can be most distracting. Your bosses will constantly want to know what's going on, there will be a myriad of suggestions on how to address the situation at hand, there will be scepticism on how matters are handled, there will be varying opinions on the way forward. As a leader – and especially an Asian leader, who can sometimes bow to the constant noise – it is important that you take charge of the situation and get everyone focused on a visible plan forward. This plan should be written down and shared, taking into consideration the points from your stakeholders, but ultimately pointing to the direction and activities that you will take to get out of the crisis. This becomes a *focusing document* that everyone can be aligned on, and more importantly, affords you the time and space to execute the time-sensitive crisis-mitigating actions. In an emergency, we need to move quickly from deliberation to action!

Win-Win Outcomes

In the 1970s, the Nobel-laureate economist Milton Friedman offered the idea that the goal of business executives was to maximise shareholder value. By the end of the 20th century, this became gospel in the business world. I recall seeing many companies' mission statements over the course of my career which outlined this singular goal of prioritising shareholder value above all else.

However, as globalisation and ensuing economic inequality took dramatic shape in most markets, there has been a call to businesses to be more balanced in serving a broader spectrum of stakeholders: shareholders (naturally), employees, suppliers, customers and the community. The Business Round Table in the U.S., endorsed by almost 200 CEOs of the largest corporations, acknowledged this approach in 2019.

The Covid-19 pandemic shone a bright spotlight on the inequity of frontline workers and disadvantaged groups. All of us in Asia, with businesses in a growth or emerging phase, have the unique opportunity to add more shape to this idea of stakeholder capitalism. We certainly need to run profitable businesses, and shareholders must get their due returns, but we can also add understanding and empathy to make human decisions, to be better partners with win-win outcomes, and to be sure we give back meaningfully to the communities in which we operate. It all makes for good, sustainable business, and our more educated and enlightened customers of the future will give us credit for it.

I have talked about how we operate in an increasingly VUCA world. And how the leadership skills I have discussed in this book would serve to help. These skills are well summarised by Bob Johansen, Distinguished Fellow of the Institute for the Future, who offers an antidote to the VUCA model. To counter Volatility, Uncertainty, Complexity and Ambiguity, leaders can guide their organisations through with Vision, Understanding, Clarity and Agility. In a crisis, great leaders don't sit back and wait for events to unfold. Great leaders take the initiative to mitigate the risks and seek opportunities to transform their businesses and organisations so that they come out the other end of the crisis even stronger.

In the words of Muhammad Ali: "Don't count the days, make the days count."

A Commitment to Change

"It is not the strongest of the species
that survive, not the most intelligent, but
the one most responsive to change."
CHARLES DARWIN

IN THIS BOOK, I have shared from an Asian leadership perspective:

- How we should reflect on some of our innate behaviours as we move up to more senior leadership roles, especially in global organisations.

- How we need to jump more into the thick of action and develop our authentic leadership voice.

- How we can bring people along with us in this new and volatile world.

But it is not enough to have read this book, pondered on some of the key points – maybe agreeing with some of them – only to then revert to your safe and comfortable posture. There must be a call to action and a sustained commitment to improving in the areas you feel you can do better as a leader. I can't emphasise this imperative enough, as Asians tend to always fall back into their comfort zones and not stretch themselves to their full potential. As a prime example of this myself, I know how big a challenge this can be. Far easier to keep the status quo.

In my many years of coaching leaders within my organisations, and now as I coach and mentor executives in other industries, the key determinant of success is not just the learning and awareness that is imparted, but the courage and commitment by leaders to try things out, see what works, and make the appropriate adjustments in style and approach. I have seen my fair share of leaders who know what to do, know where their blind spots are, but choose to remain on the easier and more comfortable path they're on. Over the years, these opportunity areas, which held them back in the past, show up time and again in their future development or performance assessments. The examples below might sound familiar to you:

- "Ahmed is too tactical, and always in the weeds. He needs to step back and see the bigger picture."

- "Chin Ann can't get her points across. I can't feel her presence or impact."

- "Robert can be a 'slavedriver' for results. While his intentions might be good, he doesn't have enough empathy for his colleagues or people, and just doesn't bring them along."

Without a commitment to change, your leadership brand will inevitably become synonymous with your leadership inadequacies. Over time, this will get firmly imprinted on you and is a stigma you will want to avoid. These leaders often give off traits of not being open to learn, not being open to feedback, and not seeking out help when help is needed – a continuation of the Heads Down approach to their own self-development.

On the opposite end of this, I have also observed my fair share of leaders who have resolved to adjust their style and approach. There is constant try-out. Not every adjustment works out for them, but they continuously seek guidance and feedback to better shape their approach. While it might reveal vulnerability, it is a good practice in my opinion to openly share the changes that you are trying to make with your supervisors, counterparts and subordinates, so that they can provide feedback and keep you on track, and to also place yourself under a bit of pressure to live up to these expectations that are laid bare in front of all of them! Because your constituents are aware of your efforts, when you ultimately succeed you will get credit for it, which positively impacts your evolving leadership brand.

A Continuous Journey

As mentioned earlier – and I hate to say it – I continue to be a prime example of an insecure Asian leader. Everything I've shared in this book comes from personal experience and showcases the areas in which I've had to overcome my shortcomings.

At the time of writing this book, I have since moved on from my executive roles to spend time as a strategic advisor, board member, and executive coach and mentor. I have also started to tick off my personal bucket list of things I wish to do more of, like music, filming, travelling, charity, and staying mentally and physically healthy. Going into these new areas doesn't come easy for me, especially after working in a structured corporate world for 30 years. I have had to set deliberate personal goals, be clear about what I want to do, and most importantly, kick myself out of my comfort zone. Throughout this transition, I have refrained from using the word "retired" (as it gives me the excuse to fall back into my safe space of inaction), but rather refer to it as a phase of moving on to new challenges and experiences.

And even now as I take on these new advisory and coaching roles, I must constantly activate my leadership muscle, and remind myself not to fall into the passive leadership traps which are innate in me as an Asian leader. Many thoughts and reflections from the learnings I've shared in this book provide timely reminders and nudges for me:

- Be courageous and raise your hand in taking on local and global board and advisory roles. Be confident in your experience and the value you can add. Don't shy away.

- Actively participate in understanding the new businesses, and make your voice heard. No silly questions, so stay engaged.

- Cheerlead the smaller startups as they accomplish the day-to-day, and put your head down to grind out the execution with them. But be clear to also keep your head up and help them map out a vision to not only win the present, but build a sustained future flow of growth.

- Provide perspective on management direction and decisions, but always push the envelope for more creative and differentiated solutions.

- Be a gatekeeper of standards, governance and excellence. While staying nimble, be sure you don't allow mediocrity to creep in.

- Remind yourself that at the higher board or advisory level, it's still not just about the numbers. Influence the health and culture of the organisation and talent, and always show appreciation.

- Influence the teams to be aware of the external environment – the opportunities to ride the megatrends, the mitigation required to deal with risks and crises.

I continue to put in the work so as to become the leader that these new roles require of me, and so that I can, in some small way, continue to be an example of an Asian leader that makes an impact and tries to punch above his weight.

In the introduction to this book, I mentioned that the ability to manage a business on a strategic level while achieving execution speed and excellence is an invaluable leadership combination that Asian leaders can aspire to. But just as important is the ability to bring stakeholders along on the journey and establish absolute trust behind the immense responsibility of the proper stewardship of the business, the brand, its capital, and the people.

Let's all dare to be different by evolving what can be a powerful Asian leadership brand. A brand that is characterised by heads up business stewardship, heads down executional prowess, evolved empathy for our stakeholders' needs, and all delivered with resilient Asian characteristics. An Asian leadership brand that wins the present and builds the future!

We have no more time to waste and have no more excuses. As Tiger Woods reminds us in his 2022 World Golf Hall of Fame induction speech: "If you don't go out there and put in the work, if you don't go out and put in the effort – one, you're not going to get the results. And two, and more importantly, you don't deserve it. You need to earn it."

NOTES

1. Khanna, P. (2019). *The Future Is Asian: Commerce, Conflict and Culture in the 21st Century*. New York: Simon & Schuster.
2. International Monetary Fund (2021). World Economic Outlook October 2021: Recovery During a Pandemic. https://www.imf.org/en/Publications/WEO/Issues/2021/10/12/world-economic-outlook-october-2021
3. Jennings, R. (2016). The F★ Word Asian Entrepreneurs Need & Why No One Likes Saying It. *Forbes*. https://www.forbes.com/sites/ralphjennings/2016/05/26/the-new-four-letter-f-word-for-asian-entrepreneurs/?sh=4c46obd632b4
4. Tsoi, G. (2015). Taipei's Fiery New Mayor Knows Whose Culture Is Best. *Foreign Policy*. https://foreignpolicy.com/2015/01/29/taipeis-fiery-new-mayor-knows-whose-culture-is-best/
5. Ana Tawfiq Husain (2020). 'In Defence of Asian Values': Investigating Lee Kuan Yew's Postcolonial 'Garrison Mentality' for the 'Singapore Story'. *Strife* 14 (Winter 2020).
6. Nardizzi, S. (2015). Leadership through Stewardship: A Foundation for Organizational Success Across Cultures. *The New York Times in Education*. https://nytimesineducation.com/spotlight/leadership-through-stewardship-a-foundation-for-organizational-success-across-cultures/
7. Linkner, J. (2010). Heads Up vs. Heads Down. *Fast Company*. https://www.fastcompany.com/1684369/heads-vs-heads-down
8. Dotlich, D.L., Cairo, P.C., Rhinesmith, S. (2006). *Head, Heart and Guts: How the World's Best Companies Develop Complete Leaders*. San Francisco: Jossey-Bass.
9. Amir Yusof (2020). How Covid-19 has disrupted the close links between Singapore and Johor. *Channel NewsAsia*. https://www.channelnewsasia.com/asia/Covid-singapore-johor-links-disruptions-rgl-pca-965476
10. For the transcript of Ghoshal's talk, visit https://empoweringpeople.nl/wordpress/wp-content/uploads/2020/05/The-smell-of-the-place.pdf
11. Standard Operating Procedure
12. Liu, Yang (2015). *East Meets West*. Cologne: Taschen.
13. VUCA World. https://www.vuca-world.org/

ACKNOWLEDGEMENTS

SPECIAL THANKS to the following people who have shaped me and helped me with the writing of this book:

My wife, Elena, who coaxed, coerced and championed the idea of penning down my experiences and learnings. Thank you for being a pillar of support and collaboration.

The leaders, bosses and supervisors I have worked for – I have learnt so much from each of you and I hope I have been a positive reflection of what you stand for.

To the colleagues and field teams that have worked with me – I owe all of you the greatest debt for your support, for trusting me to lead, and for the space to improve.

To Pearlin Siow, and her BossOfMe team, who provided great insight, and helped me better structure and shape this book to completion.

ABOUT THE AUTHOR

KENNETH CHAN is a seasoned CEO and organisation leader with close to 30 years of hands-on experience in Fortune 500 consumer and retail multinational companies such  as McDonald's, PepsiCo, Procter & Gamble and Singapore Airlines.

Kenneth was McDonald's Chief Executive Officer for China and Division President for the Greater China region between 2009 and 2015. He led an organisation of 150,000 employees and oversaw the fastest period of expansion at that time (opening over 1,000 restaurants in the span of five years) and more importantly laid a strong foundation – in organisation, talent development, supply chain, systems and tools, IT and digital transformation, branding – that has paved the way for continued, sustainable growth.

More recently, from 2016 to 2021, Kenneth served as an equity and operating partner (as part of the Lionhorn Group, McDonald's licensee) for McDonald's Singapore and Malaysia, and the Managing Director of McDonald's Singapore.

He guided the organisation successfully through the Covid-19 pandemic with a grounded resilience plan that resulted in keeping everyone safe, jobs and wages secure, and customers appreciating the brand even more.

Kenneth previously also led the McDonald's Singapore business prior to China as its Managing Director (2004–2008) while having simultaneous regional responsibilities for South Korea, Taiwan and Malaysia. In his time in Singapore, McDonald's was recognised as the Aon Hewitt Best Employer three consecutive times, and Kenneth led this winning local organisation in achieving record revenue, profit, and share growth since its 20 years of business inception.

Kenneth has also held regional and in-market brand positions in PepsiCo International and Procter & Gamble, grounding his foundation in consumer-facing businesses. He started his career in Singapore Airlines in International Relations, after completing his national service responsibilities as an officer in the Singapore Armed Forces.

He was conferred the prestigious Overseas CEO Award at the Singapore Business Awards (2014), as well as the Leading CEO Award by the Singapore Human Resources Institute (2007), and Champion of HR by HRM Magazine (2008). He now serves as a strategic advisor and executive mentor.

To continue the conversation on Asian leadership, and to provide any feedback, insights or comments, please visit www.asiansincharge.com